2084

2084

ARTIFICIAL INTELLIGENCE AND THE FUTURE OF HUMANITY

JOHN C. LENNOX

ZONDERVAN REFLECTIVE

2084

Copyright © 2020 by John C. Lennox

ISBN 978-0-310-10956-3 (hardcover)
ISBN 978-0-310-10959-4 (audio)
ISBN 978-0-310-10958-7 (ebook)

Published in association with the literary agency of Mark Sweeney & Associates, Chicago, Illinois 60611.

Cover design: Studio Gearbox
Cover photo: © Juergen Faelchle; Raevsky Lab; Omelchenko/Shutterstock
Interior design: Kait Lamphere

Printed and bound in the UK using 100% Renewable Electricity at CPI Group (UK) Ltd

24 24 25 26 27 28 29 30 31 32 /CPI/ 15 14 13 12 11 10 9 8 7

To all grandchildren, including my own ten –
Janie Grace, Herbie, Freddie, Sally, Lizzie, Jessica,
Robin, Rowan, Jonah, and Jesse –
in the hope that it will help them
face the challenges of an AI-dominated world.

CONTENTS

PREFACE

This book represents an attempt to address questions of where humanity is going in terms of technological enhancement, bio-engineering, and, in particular, artificial intelligence. Will we be able to construct artificial life and superintelligence? Will humans so modify themselves that they become something else entirely, and if so, what implications do advances in AI have on our worldviews in general and on the God question in particular?

I hope that my Orwellian title does not sound too pretentious, firstly because my book is not a dystopian novel and secondly because I am not George Orwell. The title was actually suggested to me by Oxford colleague Professor Peter Atkins when we were on our way to speak on opposite sides in a university debate entitled "Can Science Explain Everything?" I am indebted to him for the idea and for several vigorous public encounters on issues of science and God.

I am also in considerable debt to a number of people, especially to Dr. Rosalind Picard of the MIT Media Laboratory for her very perceptive comments. Others include Professor

David Cranston, Professor Danny Crookes, Professor Jeremy Gibbons, Dr. David Glass, and my ever-helpful research assistant, Dr. Simon Wenham.

My own professional background is in mathematics and the philosophy of science, not in AI, and the reader, especially if an expert in the field, may be puzzled that I appear to be invading their ground. I hasten to explain that my intention lies elsewhere. It seems to me that there are different levels of involvement in and relationship to AI. There are the pioneer thinkers, and then there are those experts who actually write the software used in AI systems. Next, we have the engineers who build the hardware. Then there are those people who understand what AI systems can do who work on developing new applications. Finally, there are writers, some scientifically trained, others not, who are interested in the significance and impact of AI – sociologically, economically, ethically.

It is clear that one does not need to know how to build an autonomous vehicle or weapon in order to have an informed view about the ethics of deploying such things. You don't need to know how to program an AI purchase tracker system in order to have a valid opinion about invasion of privacy.

In fact, there is great interest among all levels of involvement in writing for the thoughtful reader at the level of the public understanding of science. It is at this level that I have pitched this book, and I am indebted to all of those people, experts in different ways, who have already written on the topic.

CHAPTER ONE

MAPPING OUT THE TERRITORY

We humans are insatiably curious. We have been asking questions since the dawn of history. We've especially been asking the big questions about origin and destiny: Where do I come from and where am I going? Their importance is obvious. Our answer to the first shapes our concepts of who we are, and our answer to the second gives us goals to live for. Taken together, our responses to these questions help frame our worldview, the narrative that gives our lives their meaning.

The problem is that these are not easy questions, as we see from the fact that many and contradictory answers are on offer. Yet, by and large, we have not let that hinder us. Over the centuries, humans have proposed some answers given by science, some by philosophy, some based on religion, others on politics, etc.

Two of the most famous futuristic scenarios are the 1931 novel *Brave New World* by Aldous Huxley and George Orwell's novel *1984*, published in 1949. Both of them have, at various times, been given very high ranking as influential English novels. For instance, Orwell's was chosen in 2005 by *Time* magazine as one of the 100 best English-language novels from 1923 to 2005. Both novels are dystopian: that is, according to the *Oxford English Dictionary*, "they describe an imaginary place or condition that is as bad as possible." However, the really bad places that they describe are very different, and their differences, which give us helpful insights that will be useful to us later, were succinctly explained by sociologist Neil Postman in his highly regarded work *Amusing Ourselves to Death*:

> Orwell warns that we will be overcome by an externally imposed oppression. But in Huxley's vision, no Big Brother is required to deprive people of their autonomy, maturity and history. As he saw it, people will come to love their oppression, to adore the technologies that undo their capacities to think.
>
> What Orwell feared were those who would ban books. What Huxley feared was there would be no reason to ban a book, for there would be no one who wanted to read one. Orwell feared those who would deprive us of information. Huxley feared those who would give us so much that we would be reduced to passivity and egoism. Orwell feared that the truth would be concealed from us. Huxley feared that the truth would be drowned in a sea of irrelevance. Orwell feared we would become a captive culture. Huxley feared we would become a trivial culture . . . In short, Orwell feared that what we hate will ruin us. Huxley feared that what we love will ruin us.[1]

Orwell introduced ideas of blanket surveillance in a totalitarian state, of "thought control" and "newspeak," ideas that nowadays increasingly come up in connection with developments in artificial intelligence (AI), particularly the attempt to build computer technology that can do the sorts of things that a human mind can do – in short, the production of an imitation mind. Billions of dollars are now being invested in the development of AI systems, and not surprisingly, there is a great deal of interest in where it is all going to lead: for instance, better quality of life through digital assistance, medical innovation, and human enhancement on the one hand, and fear of job losses and Orwellian surveillance societies on the other hand.

Even the pope is getting involved. In September 2019, he sounded a warning that the race to create artificial intelligence and other forms of digital development pose the risk of increasing social inequality unless the work is accompanied by an ethical evaluation of the common good. He said: "If technological advancement became the cause of increasingly evident inequalities, it would not be true and real progress. If mankind's so-called technological progress were to become an enemy of the common good, this would lead to an unfortunate regression to a form of barbarism dictated by the law of the strongest."[2]

Most of the successes so far in AI have to do with building systems that do one thing that normally takes human intelligence to implement. However, on the more speculative side – certainly at the moment – there is great interest in the vastly more ambitious quest to build systems that can do all that human intelligence can do, that is, artificial general intelligence (AGI), which some think will surpass human intelligence within a relatively short time, certainly by 2084 or even earlier, according to some speculations. Some imagine that AGI, if we ever get there, will function as a god, while others, as a totalitarian despot.

As I looked for a way to introduce these burgeoning topics and the hopes and fears they generate, three contemporary bestselling books came to my attention. The first two are written by Israeli historian Yuval Noah Harari – *Sapiens: A Brief History of Humankind*, which deals, as its title suggests, with the first of our questions, the origins of humanity, and *Homo Deus: A Brief History of Tomorrow*, which deals with humanity's future. The third book, *Origin* by Dan Brown, is a novel, like Huxley's and Orwell's. It focusses on the use of AI to answer both of our questions in the form of a page-turning thriller that is likely to be read by millions of people, if Brown's mind-boggling sales figures run true to form. It is likely, therefore, to impact the thinking of many people, particularly the young. Because the book reflects the admitted questionings of its author on these issues, it forms an intriguing springboard for our own exploration.

In addition, I am aware that science fiction has been a stimulus to some people in getting them started on a useful career in science itself. However, a word of caution is appropriate here. Brown claims to use real science to come to his conclusions, and so, in spite of the fact that his book is a work of fiction, we shall have to be careful to test his arguments and conclusions for truth content.

That is especially important since he says that his basic motivation for writing was to tackle the question, "Will God survive science?" It was this same question in various forms that has motivated me to write several of my books. That work has led me to the conclusion that God will more than survive science, but it has also led me seriously to question whether atheism will survive science.[3]

One of Dan Brown's main characters in *Origin* is a billionaire computer scientist and artificial intelligence expert, Edmond Kirsch, who claims to have solved the questions of life's origin and human destiny. He intends to use his results to fulfil his long-time goal to "employ the truth of science to destroy the myth of religions,"[4] meaning, in particular, the three Abrahamic faiths: Judaism, Christianity, and Islam. Perhaps inevitably, he concentrates on Christianity. His solutions, when they are eventually revealed to the world, are a product of his expertise in artificial intelligence. His take on the future involves the technological modification of human beings.

It should be pointed out right away that it is not only historians and science fiction writers but some of our most respected scientists who are suggesting that humanity itself may be changed by technology. For instance, UK Astronomer Royal Lord Rees says, "We can have zero confidence that the dominant intelligences a few centuries hence will have any emotional resonance with us – even though they may have an algorithmic understanding of how we behaved."[5]

In the same vein, Rees also said: "Abstract thinking by biological brains has underpinned the emergence of all culture and science. But this activity – spanning tens of millennia at most – will be a brief precursor to the more powerful intellects of the inorganic post-human era. So, in the far future, it won't be the minds of humans, but those of machines, that will most fully understand the cosmos."[6]

This is a topic that is not going to go away. It is of interest not only to people who are directly involved in AI research but also to mathematicians and scientists in other disciplines whose work and outlook are increasingly impacted by it. Indeed, since the outcomes and ideas surrounding work on AI will inevitably affect us all, many people are thinking and writing about it who are not scientists at all. The implications are such that it is important that, for instance, philosophers, ethicists, theologians, cultural commentators, novelists, and artists get involved in the wider debate. After all, you do not need to be a nuclear physicist or climatologist in order to discuss the impact of nuclear energy or climate change.

WHAT IS AI?

Let us start by thinking about robots. The word *robot* derives from a Czech (and Russian) word for *work – robota*. A robot is a machine designed and programmed by an intelligent human to do, typically, a single task that involves interaction with its physical environment, a task that would normally require an intelligent human being to do it. In that sense, its behaviour simulates human intelligence, a circumstance that has given rise to considerable debate as to whether or not it itself should be considered in some sense intelligent, even if that intelligence is not what we understand human intelligence to be – another large question in itself.

The term *AI* was coined in a summer school held at the mathematics department of Dartmouth University in 1956 that was organised by John McCarthy, who said, "AI is the science and engineering of making intelligent machines."[7]

The term is now used both for the intelligent machines that are the goal and for the science and technology that are aiming at that goal.

Research in this area has taken two main directions. Broadly speaking, firstly, there is the attempt to understand human reasoning and thought processes by modelling them using computer technology, and, secondly, there is the study of human behaviour and the attempt to construct machinery that will imitate it. The difference is important – it is one thing to make a machine that can simulate, say, a human hand lifting an object; it is a completely different thing to make a machine that can simulate the thoughts of a human when he or she is lifting an object. It is much easier to do the first than the second, and if utility is all that is required, then the first is all that is necessary. After all, the aircraft industry involves making machines that fly, but it does not involve constructing an electronic brain like that of a bird in order for the aircraft to fly in exactly the same way as birds do – by flapping its wings.[8]

The idea of constructing machines that can simulate aspects of human and, indeed, animal behaviour has a long history. Two thousand years ago, the Greek mathematician Heron of Alexandria constructed a basin adorned with mechanical singing birds and an owl that could turn its head and make the birds go quiet. Through the centuries, people became fascinated with making automata, machines that replicated some aspect of life. An impressive collection of very sophisticated examples of such automata can be seen, for example, in the London Science Museum, the Kunsthistorisches Museum in Vienna, and the Museum Speelklok in Utrecht. Interest in constructing such machines declined in the nineteenth century but continued to live on in fiction – like the 1818 novel *Frankenstein* by Mary Wollstonecraft Shelley. It has been a staple diet of science fiction since the beginning of that genre.

One of the important human activities in everyday life is numerical calculation, and a great deal of effort has been made to automate this process. In the seventeenth century, French mathematician Blaise Pascal made a mechanical calculator,[9] which he designed in order to help his father, a tax official, with tedious calculations. In the nineteenth century, Charles Babbage laid the foundations of programmable computation by first inventing the difference engine – an automatic adding machine – and then the analytical engine, which was the first programmable calculator. He is rightly regarded as the father of the modern computer.

During the Second World War, the brilliant British computer scientist Alan Turing used sophisticated electronic computer technology to build equipment, notably the Bombe, which enabled him and his team at Bletchley Park to decipher the German "Enigma" code that was used for secret military communications. Turing's inventions and theoretical work led to his proposal of a "learning machine." According to him, a machine that could converse with humans – without the humans knowing that it is a machine – would win the "imitation game" and could be said to be "intelligent." Now known as the Turing Test, this definition provided a practical test for attributing intelligence to a machine. However, as we shall later see, this approach has met serious challenges from philosophers.

Around the same time (1951), Marvin Minsky (co-founder of MIT's AI research laboratory) and Dean Edmonds build the first neural network computer. Subsequent landmark achievements that attracted huge public attention were IBM's Deep Blue computer beating world chess champion Garry Kasparov in 1997, and in 2016 Google's AlphaGo program becoming the first to beat an unhandicapped professional human Go player using machine learning. The importance of AI has been recognised by the 2018 Turing Award, known as the "Nobel Prize of Computing," which was given to a trio of researchers who laid the foundations for the current boom in artificial intelligence, particularly in the subfield of deep learning.

Early robots and AI systems did not involve what is now called "machine learning." Key to the current machine learning process is the idea of an algorithm, which may be of various types – e.g., symbolic, mathematical, etc.[10] The word *algorithm* is derived from the name of a famous Persian mathematician, astronomer, and geographer, Muḥammad ibn Mūsā al-Khwārizmī (ca. 780–850).[11]

Nowadays an algorithm is "a precisely defined set of mathematical or logical operations for the performance of a particular task" (*OED*). The concept can be traced to ancient Babylonia in 1800–1600 BC. Eminent computer scientist Donald Knuth of Stanford University published some of these early algorithms and concluded, "The calculations described in Babylonian tablets are not merely the solutions to specific individual problems; they are actually general procedures for solving a whole class of problems."[12] And that is the key feature of an algorithm: once you know how it works, you can solve not only one problem but a whole class of problems.

One of the most famous examples that many of us met in school is the Euclidian algorithm, which is a procedure used to find the greatest common divisor (GCD) of two positive integers or numbers. It was first described by Euclid in his manuscript *The Elements*, written around 300 BC. It is an efficient algorithm that, in some form or other, is still used by computers today. Its implementation involves the successive division and calculation of remainders until the desired result is reached. The operation of the algorithm is best grasped by following an example – although the vital point is that it works for any pair of integers.

Suppose we wish to calculate the GCD of 56 and 12. We would follow these steps:

1. Step 1: Divide the larger number by the smaller.
   - $56 \div 12 = 4$ with remainder 8
2. Step 2: Divide the dividing number, 12, by the remainder from the previous step.
   - $12 \div 8 = 1$ with remainder 4
3. Step 3: Continue step 2 until no remainders are left (in this case there is only one more step).
   - $8 \div 4 = 2$ (no remainder)

In this case, the GCD is 4.

It is easy to translate this into software code and implement it on a computer. A glance online will show that there are thousands of different kinds of algorithms in use today in every conceivable branch of science, engineering, and medicine. Robotics is a prime example, as robots are usually specifically designed to perform a single task again and again and again.

In a typical contemporary AI system, the relevant algorithms are embedded in computer software that sorts, filters, and selects various pieces of data that are presented to it. One approach attempts to simulate, at least to some degree, the neuronal functions in the human cortex (neural networks). In general terms, such a system can use training data to "learn" (machine learning[13]) to recognise, identify, and interpret digital patterns such as images, sound, speech, text, or data. Another approach uses computer applications involving Bayesian probability logic to analyse the available information from a statistical perspective in order to estimate the likelihood of a particular hypothesis. In short, a machine learning system takes in information about the past and makes decisions or predictions when it is presented with new information.

It is important to note that the algorithms themselves are explicitly programmed to perform function approximation, usually via numerical optimization, and in most cases, they are also explicitly given examples of inputs and outputs and stopping criteria to guide the optimization. They don't "crunch" without a human in the loop at some level guiding the whole process (even if the human builds a "critic" algorithm and inserts it into the loop, etc.). The human involvement is conscious. The machine is not.

In a lot of early work in AI, humans explicitly devised an algorithm to solve a particular problem. In more recent AI, they do not. Instead, they devise a general learning algorithm, which then "learns" a solution to the problem. Often the human developers don't know an explicit algorithm for solving the problem and don't know how the system arrives at its conclusions. Early chess-playing programs were of the first type (even Deep Blue was more in this category), whereas the modern Go software is of the second type.

Here are some examples of AI systems, many of them already familiar to the public:

- Amazon uses algorithms that trace all the products you and millions of other people buy from them online. It then sifts through this vast database and compares the list with other similar products that you do not yet have. Finally, it uses statistical methods to select those products that are bought by people "like you" and causes them to pop up on your screen.
- A computer-based algorithm can sort through a database consisting of job applications and suggest the applicant most suited to the job. Jobs that attract many thousands of applications now are the subject of AI systems that conduct the first interviews where data is not only gathered about candidates' answers to questions, but their emotional reactions are also filmed and sifted in order to determine their suitability for an interview.
- AI is being successfully applied to the design of more energy-efficient buildings, household appliances connected by the Internet of Things, and integrated transport systems.
- AI systems are already up and running that work with a database consisting of many thousands of X-rays of lungs, say, in various states of health, together with top-level professional medical analysis of their state of health. The system then compares an X-ray of your lungs with the database in order to check whether or not you have, say, a specific type of cancer. More specifically, it tends to extract statistics about visual patterns in the X-ray image and compare these to other extracted patterns in the

database. Such systems can now make diagnoses in some cases with better accuracy than the best human doctors.

- Astronomers have used AI to train machine learning to identify Fast Radio Bursts from distant galaxies by sifting through a massive database of signals collected from radio telescopes. They have already (September 2018) found seventy-two new examples that they will now investigate in their SETI research. They are also using AI for automated galaxy recognition.

- Autonomous vehicles, since they are unconscious machines, raise immediate ethical problems regarding the principles to be built into them as to what they should try to avoid. It is interesting to note that the autopilot system in an aircraft has not been made fully autonomous, even though one might argue that aircraft are easier to fly than self-driving cars. The reason may well be that the companies that fly them want to stay in business, because there really is no ethical issue as to who would be responsible if the plane crashed, no matter if it killed some people to save others.

- Facial recognition is now highly developed. One rather amusing application is to use AI face recognition technology in a pub in order to recognise who is next in line to get a drink at the bar and so avoid unfair queue jumping. CCTV cameras are now ubiquitous and are used by police to track criminal activity. However, such surveillance systems can also be used for social control. We shall look later at the major ethical issues that arise from such applications.

- Autonomous weapons and the related ethical problems are the subject of international debate.

It is obvious from even this short list that many, if not all, of these developments raise ethical questions from financial manipulation and crime to invasion of privacy and social control. The danger is that people are carried away with the "if it can be done, it should be done" mentality without thinking carefully through potential ethical problems. However, it must be said that ethical issues are now rapidly rising in importance on the agenda of leading players in the AI world. The big question to be faced is: How can an ethical dimension be built into an algorithm that is itself devoid of heart, soul, and mind?

It is important to realise that most AI systems, such as those above, are usually designed to do just one thing, such as drive a car, diagnose an illness, or make predictions based on the past. To keep that in mind, the term *narrow AI* is often used. However, since all applications of AI to date are narrow, some people prefer to use the term *cognitive technologies* to cover what has been achieved so far in the quest for the intelligent machine.

Nick Bostrom and Eliezer Yudkowsky comment:

Current AI algorithms with human-equivalent or -superior performance are characterized by a deliberately-programmed competence only in a single, restricted domain. Deep Blue became the world champion at chess, but it cannot even play checkers, let alone drive a car or make a scientific discovery. Such modern AI algorithms resemble all biological life with the sole exception of *Homo sapiens*. A bee exhibits competence at building hives; a beaver exhibits competence at building dams; but a bee doesn't build dams, and a beaver can't learn to build a hive. A human, watching, can learn to do both; but this is a unique ability among biological lifeforms.[14]

One potential (further) source of confusion in the discussion is that by using everyday words like *learning*, *planning*, *reasoning*, and *intelligence* as technical terms to describe inanimate machinery, some computer scientists make AI systems sound more capable than they actually are, since they often use such terms in a much narrower way than common use. As a result, media coverage of AI tends to over-dramatise results and be overly optimistic or overly fearful. Professor of Computer Engineering Danny Crookes of Queens University Belfast writes:

> The current technologies which are beginning to worry people because of their power to monitor and manipulate whole populations are actually not very intelligent. Indeed, they don't have to be. Their power lies in their ability to handle vast amounts of data, to build up a profile of individuals, and to detect patterns, both within an individual's behaviour and across a population. The Nazis and Communist states did this manually on a smaller scale. The technology now exists to do the same thing on a global scale. That's worrying, or impressive, but it is not really intelligence. So-called "deep learning" is now all the rage in AI research, but there's nothing particularly new in it: it's just that the computing power now exists to run the multi-layer (deep) neural networks which have existed on paper for decades.[15]

Professor Joseph McRae Mellichamp of the University of Alabama, speaking at a conference at Yale University to an audience that contained the Nobel Prize winner Sir John Eccles, famous for his discovery of the synapse, together with a number of the pioneers of AI, said: "It seems to me that a lot of needless debate could be avoided if AI researchers would admit that there are fundamental differences between machine intelligence and human intelligence – differences that cannot be overcome by any amount of research." In other words, to cite the succinct title of Mellichamp's talk, "'the artificial' in artificial intelligence is real."[16]

Professor Crookes stresses the need for realism here:

We are still a long, long way from creating real human-like intelligence. People have been fooled by the impact of data-driven computing (as in the above paragraph) into thinking that we are approaching the level of human intelligence. But in my opinion, we are nowhere near it. Indeed, it might be argued that progress in real AI in recent years has actually slowed down. There is probably less research into real AI now than before, because most of the funding is geared essentially to advertising! Researchers follow the money.

There are huge challenges in our understanding of the human reasoning process. For what it's worth, I see two fundamental problems yet to be cracked: (1) Even if we knew the rules of human reasoning, how do we abstract from a physical situation to a more abstract formulation so that we can apply the general rules of reasoning? (2) How can a computer build up and hold an internal mental model of the real world? Think of how a blind person visualises the world and reasons about it. Humans have

26

the general-purpose ability to visualise things and to reason about scenarios of objects and processes that exist only in our minds. This general-purpose capability, which humans all have, is phenomenal; it is a key requirement for real intelligence, but it is fundamentally lacking in AI systems. There are reasons to doubt if we will ever get there.

I suppose my point is that we need to be careful about even assuming that humanity has the intellectual capability to create an intelligence rivalling human intelligence, let alone superseding it, no matter how much time we have.[17]

We need to keep this very clearly in mind as we look at the way in which Dan Brown employs (narrow) AI in his novel to tackle his two big philosophical questions.

NOTES

1. Neil Postman, *Amusing Ourselves to Death: Public Discourse in the Age of Show Business*, 20th anniv. ed. (1986; repr., New York: Penguin, 2006), xix–xx.

2. "The Pope Warns Tech Companies to Use AI for 'Common Good,'" *Time*, 27 September 2019, https://time.com/5688191/pope-francis-artificial-intelligence-common-good.

3. I shall use the term *atheism* in its widest sense to denote the rejection of the idea of a creator God.

4. Dan Brown, *Origin* (New York: Doubleday, 2017), 53.

5. Martin Rees, *On the Future: Prospects for Humanity* (Princeton, NJ: Princeton University Press, 2018), 7.

6. Martin Rees, "Astronomer Royal Martin Rees: How Soon Will Robots Take Over the World?" *The Telegraph*, 23 May 2015, www.telegraph.co.uk/culture/hay-festival/11605785/Astronomer-Royal-Martin-Rees-predicts-the-world-will-be-run-by-computers-soon.html.

7. John McCarthy, "What Is Artificial Intelligence?" www-formal.stanford.edu/jmc/whatisai.pdf.

8. See Stuart Russell and Peter Norvig, eds., *Artificial Intelligence: A Modern Approach*, 3rd ed. (Harlow: Pearson Education, 2016), 1–5.

9. The first known calculating machine was made around 1623 by German professor of Hebrew and astronomy Wilhelm Schickard.

10. It should be noted that early AI systems did not use algorithms.

11. See the delightful article in the *BMJ Opinion* by my Oxford colleague Jeffrey Aronson, "When I Use a Word . . . Algorithms," *BMJ Opinion*, 11 August 2017, https://blogs.bmj.com/bmj/2017/08/11/jeffrey-aronson-when-i-use-a-word-algorithms.

12. Donald E. Knuth, "Ancient Babylonian Algorithms," *Communications of the ACM*, vol. 15, issue 7 (July 1972): 672–73.

13. The *Encyclopedia of Artificial Intelligence* defines machine learning as "an area of Artificial Intelligence dealing with adaptive computational methods such as Artificial Neural Networks and Genetic Algorithms" (Juan Ramon Rabunal Dopico, Julian Dorado de la Calle, and Alejandro Pazos Sierra, eds., *Encyclopedia of Artificial Intelligence* [Hershey, PA: Information Service Reference, 2009], 666).

14. Nick Bostrom and Eliezer Yudkowsky, "The Ethics of Artificial Intelligence," in *Cambridge Handbook of Artificial Intelligence*, ed. Keith Frankish and William M. Ramsey (Cambridge: Cambridge University Press, 2014), 318.

15. Private communication (2019). Used with permission.

16. Private communication (2018) by the author of a paper presented at the Artificial Intelligence and Human Mind conference (Yale University, 1986). Used with permission. An interesting report on the conference can be found here: www.aaai.org/ojs/index.php/aimagazine/article/view/601.

17. Private communication (2019). Used with permission.

CHAPTER TWO

FIRST BIG QUESTION: WHERE DO WE COME FROM?

The fictional professor Edmond Kirsch of Dan Brown's novel *Origin* revisits the famous experiment that chemists Stanley Miller and Harold Urey performed in 1953, which won them the Nobel Prize. They mixed various chemicals, such as hydrogen, methane, and ammonia, thought to exist in the early earth atmosphere, in a test tube and applied an electric spark. As the chemical mixture settled down, they found in it some of the amino acids that are often called the building blocks for life. For a time, their work was hailed as a scientific solution to the problem of the origin of life, but as time went on, it was realised that the experiment did not deliver – it produced only a few of the amino acids necessary.

However, the test tubes used in the experiment were preserved, and the experiment was revisited more than fifty years later, leading to the following results published by six authors in the October edition of *Science* (2008) under the title "The Miller Volcanic Spark Discharge Experiment." We should note that Dan Brown correctly states that this is actual published scientific work and not fiction. Here is the abstract of that paper:

Miller's 1950s experiments used, besides the apparatus known in textbooks, one that generated a hot water mist in the spark flask, simulating a water vapor-rich volcanic eruption. We found the original extracts of this experiment in Miller's material and reanalyzed them. The volcanic apparatus produced a wider variety of amino acids than the classic one. Release of reduced gases in volcanic eruptions accompanied by lightning could have been common on the early Earth. Prebiotic compounds synthesized in these environments could have locally accumulated, where they could have undergone further processing.[1]

This research forms the trigger to the idea that Dan Brown develops in his novel. The Miller-Urey experiment was a simulation carried out in the laboratory long before the days of computer modelling. What Brown's fictitious AI expert does is to set up a mathematical model of the Miller-Urey experiment, factoring in the new information from 2008 and paying much more attention to the detailed interactions of chemicals down to the molecular level and thus securing a huge amount of data of the sort that AI systems are ideal at processing. He runs the experiment in virtual reality. It fails at first until he adjusts it to take into account entropy, which is the tendency for everything in the universe to run down towards equilibrium – your cup of hot coffee dissipates its heat to its surroundings and cools down but will never heat up again. The rerun eventually – lo and behold! – produces the double helix of DNA. Life is generated by natural processes without supernatural intervention. The problem is solved.

Well, certainly in the *novel* it is solved, and in such a page-turning way that will intrigue many readers. But the question of the origin of life is a real question of such importance that we need to investigate it a lot more in order to disentangle fact from fiction. Firstly, because in the novel (and often in real life) we are not dealing here with science pure and simple but with a scientist whose science is influenced by his worldview – in Kirsch's case, atheism. He expresses it by saying: "The age of religion is drawing to an end . . . and the age of science is dawning"[2] – which view, rather unsurprisingly, appears to coincide with that of Dan Brown.

The first disturbing thing about all of this alleged use of recent science is that the lead author of the 2008 article on which Brown bases his argument, this time a real scientist, Jeremy England of MIT, neither shares Brown's worldview nor approves of Brown's use of his research. We will let professor England speak for himself. Here is what he had to say about Dan Brown's book to the *Wall Street Journal* of October 12, 2017 – his first sentence representing the substance of what he thinks:

> There's no real science in the book to argue over . . . I'm a scientist, but I also study and live by the Hebrew Bible. To me, the idea that physics could prove that the God of Abraham is not the creator and ruler of the world reflects a serious misunderstanding – of both the scientific method and the function of the biblical text.[3]

England goes on to point out that science is not capable of disproving an explanatory matrix that sees confirmation of the activity of a creator in what we find in nature.

Dan Brown's *Origin* is, therefore, from a scientific perspective, flawed from the start by making the dubious move of citing someone's scientific research to make plausible the exact opposite of what the scientist himself thinks that it means. One may of course argue that this is a novel; it is fiction, and so Brown has the freedom to do what he likes. Maybe, but the danger is that, since Brown says he is motivated by a serious philosophical question, many people may well believe what he says, thinking that his conclusions are in tune with established science.

Not only that, but the claim that the simulation in Kirsch's scenario produced virtual DNA, and therefore solved the problem of life's origin, is pure science fiction. From the perspective of actual science, it is not even remotely plausible. One of the world's top experts on the chemistry of the origin of life, indeed one of the current most influential scientists in the world, James Tour, professor of chemistry, nanotechnology, and computer science at Houston's Rice University, has no doubt that chemistry invalidates Brown's claims:

Life should not exist. This much we know from chemistry. In contrast to the ubiquity of life on earth, the lifelessness of other planets makes far better chemical sense . . .

Consider the following *gedankenexperiment*. Let us assume that *all* the molecules we think may be needed to construct a cell are available in the requisite chemical and stereochemical purities. Let us assume that these molecules can be separated and delivered to a well-equipped laboratory. Let us also assume that the millions of articles comprising the chemical and biochemical literature are readily accessible.

How might we build a cell?

It is not enough to have the chemicals on hand. The relationship between the nucleotides and everything else must be specified and, for this, coding information is essential. DNA and RNA are the primary informational carriers of the cell. No matter the medium life might have adopted at the very beginning, its information had to come from somewhere. A string of nucleotides does not inherently encode anything. Let us assume that DNA and RNA are available in whatever sequence we desire.[4]

We should note that, for the sake of the argument, James Tour is even granting Edmond Kirsch his (virtual) DNA, even though that involves the deep problem of the origin of the information content of DNA since there is no evidence that it is derivable from chemistry by mindless, unguided processes. That immense problem notwithstanding, Tour's detailed chemical investigation contradicts the claims made by Kirsch: "We synthetic chemists should state the obvious. The appearance of life on earth is a mystery. We are nowhere near solving this problem. The proposals offered thus far to explain life's origin make no scientific sense."[5]

That is the verdict of science.

Kirsch's fictitious verdict arises from his atheistic philosophy. Science does not support it. Also, in any case, fatal to Kirsch's "case" is his false conviction that the laws of nature can do the job of producing life. He is not the only one to think so. Another example of this basic misunderstanding of the nature of law is given by well-known physicist Paul Davies who said: "There's no need to invoke anything supernatural in the origins of the universe or of life. I have never liked the idea of divine tinkering. For me it is much more inspiring to believe that a set of mathematical laws can be so clever as to bring all these things into being."[6]

However, in the world in which most of us live, the simple law of arithmetic by itself, $1 + 1 = 2$, never brought anything into being. It certainly has never put any money into my bank account. If I put £1,000 into the bank, and later another £1,000, the laws of arithmetic will rationally explain how it is that I now have £2,000 in the bank. But if I never put any money into the bank myself and simply leave it to the laws of arithmetic to bring money into being in my bank account, I shall remain permanently bankrupt.

C. S. Lewis grasped this issue with characteristic clarity. Of the events that combine to make up history, he writes: "To think the laws can produce it is like thinking that you can create real money by simply doing sums."[7] The world of strict naturalism, in which clever mathematical laws all by themselves bring the universe and life into existence, is pure (science) fiction. Theories and laws do not bring matter/energy into existence. The view that nevertheless they somehow have that capacity seems a rather desperate refuge from the alternative rational possibility that there was a Creator.

Clearly Davies, Kirsch, and Brown are unaware that the laws of nature do not actually *explain* the world to us. What they do is *describe* its regularities. Not only that, but the laws of nature do not even *cause* anything, and hence they do not *create* anything. A moment's thought will convince you that Newton's laws of motion have never moved a billiard ball in the history of the universe, let alone created the ball to start with. The laws describe the motion once the ball is there and has been set in movement by a person wielding a billiard cue.

Dan Brown's AI genius, Kirsch, clearly does not understand this. However, even if you ignore this (vital) point, you are faced with a further question, which, to his credit, Brown does in fact flag up by putting it into the mouth of his well-known hero, Harvard professor of symbology Robert Langdon. Brown writes: "Edmond's discovery was enthralling and clearly incendiary, but for Langdon it raised one burning question that he was surprised nobody was asking: *If the laws of physics are so powerful that they can create life . . . who created the laws?*" The narrative continues: "The question, of course, resulted in a dizzying intellectual hall of mirrors and brought everything full circle."[8]

But does it? Presumably Brown means that if you ask who created the laws, then you will logically have to ask who created that creator, and so on forever. Richard Dawkins puts this forward in *The God Delusion* as a knock-down argument against the existence of a creator God. However, it is no such thing. For if we ask the question who created the creator, we are *assuming* that the creator is created. But according to the biblical worldview, the Creator, God, is not created but is eternal. Therefore, the time sequence–dependent question that assumes there is something before God that created God therefore does not even apply to him!

It does, however, apply to things that are not eternal, so I put it to Dawkins: "You believe the universe created you.

35

Who, then, created your creator?" I have waited over a decade and still no reply. I am tempted to think that this is a case of hoist with your own petard.

For there is no "dizzying intellectual hall of mirrors" here, nor does such reasoning bring "everything full circle." No, the question where the laws come from has been asked and given a perfectly intelligible answer by the very greatest of scientists – men like Galileo, Kepler, Newton, and Clerk Maxwell, all of whom, like James Tour and Jeremy England, are believers in God. They conclude that the laws came from God, and that conviction inspired their science. C. S. Lewis, summarising the work of the eminent philosopher and historian of science Sir Alfred North Whitehead, expressed it as follows: "Men became scientific because they expected Law in Nature, and they expected Law in Nature because they believed in a Legislator."[9]

Far from hindering the rise of modern science, faith in God was the motor that drove it. It is sad, therefore, that many people will think that Brown has shown that science has buried God, not because of the logic or science behind his argument, but because his readers are carried along to that conclusion by the emotional intensity of a blockbuster thriller. How can it be wrong, since it makes science so exciting?

Later in the book we discover that Kirsch had dreamed not so much of abolishing religion but rather to "create a *new* religion – a universal belief that united people rather than divided them. He thought that if he could convince people to revere the natural universe and the laws of physics that created us, then every culture would celebrate the same creation story rather than go to war over which of their antique myths was the most accurate."[10]

This is no new idea. For instance, the "science as religion" idea was promoted by atheist T. H. Huxley, who wished to turn churches into temples to the goddess Sophia (wisdom), with scientists as its priests. However, there is no future in a religion based on the completely false notion that the laws of nature created us and the universe. In more recent years, Darwinism (or some version of it) appears to function as a religion. This is argued by philosopher of biology Michael Ruse in his book *Darwinism as Religion*.[11]

There is more to be said. The late Stephen Hawking seemed to keep a door open for God in the last paragraph of his best-seller *A Brief History of Time*, although he closed it some years later in another bestseller, *The Grand Design*, where he clearly asserted his atheism. I get the impression that Dan Brown's *Origin* more than leaves a door open for God, presumably deliberately. For its fictional hero Robert Langdon hesitates to accept Edmond Kirsch's thesis uncritically. The reasons given are important and are revealed when the equally fictional highly intelligent director of the Guggenheim Museum, Ambra Vidal, asks Langdon about God. Langdon's reply to her is that "for me the question of God lies in understanding the difference between codes and patterns . . . Patterns occur everywhere in nature . . . codes do not occur naturally in the world . . . Codes are the deliberate inventions of intelligent consciousness."[12]

She then mentions DNA, which is a superb example of chemical coding in that the DNA molecule consists of a "word" in a four "letter" chemical "alphabet." At 3.4 billion letters, it is the longest word that has ever been discovered. Langdon then goes on to confirm what many of us (including the author) have long since thought, that this is powerful evidence of a divine signature. As a mathematician, I was both surprised – given Brown's overall thesis – and delighted to read Langdon's conclusion: "When I witness the precision of mathematics, the reliability of physics, and the symmetries of the cosmos, I don't feel like I'm observing cold science; I feel as if I'm seeing a living footprint . . . the shadow of some greater force that is just beyond our grasp."[13]

Donald Knuth, one of the fathers of computation and a Christian, said: "I think people who write programs do have at least a glimmer of extra insight into the nature of God . . . because creating a program often means that you have to create a small universe."[14]

The very same DNA that Kirsch claims to have "discovered" in his AI simulation is a code and not simply a pattern. It carries information, so it cannot have arisen by unguided natural processes as Kirsch says. The genetic code is only a paradox for those people who assume that DNA arose by unguided natural processes. The suggestion that DNA was created by an intelligence is dangerous only to atheism, not to science.

Langdon's fictional reaction mirrors that of the late real-life eminent philosopher Antony Flew, a lifelong atheist who, however, eventually abandoned his atheism and came to acknowledge the existence of God. He gave as the reason for his conversion the fact that biologists' investigation of DNA "has shown, by the almost unbelievable complexity of the arrangements which are needed to produce [life], that intelligence must have been involved." He added: "My whole life has been guided by the principle of Plato's Socrates: 'Follow the evidence, wherever it leads.'" He was asked: "What if your belief upsets people?" "That's too bad," said Flew.[15]

Indeed, the very facts that science can be done, that the universe is to an impressive extent mathematically intelligible, and that information bearing macromolecules like DNA exist are entirely consistent with, and indeed point towards, the validity of the biblical statement: "In the beginning was the Word . . . and the Word was God . . . All things were made through him" (John 1:1, 3). It is perfectly rational to say, as Francis Collins did at the announcement of the completion of the Human Genome Project under his direction, that DNA is "God's language."[16]

What are we, then, to make of Dan Brown's book and indeed of Dan Brown himself? He claims to have lost his Christian faith and is moving towards atheism, although he says he has not made that final step. Like his character Edmond Kirsch, he believes that the laws of nature can explain life. He calls his views conflicted. The book bears that out. At times, it seems to endorse atheism, and yet towards the end, the notion that there is an intelligent designer God behind the universe is given credibility. At other times, the book appears to approve of the destruction of religion by science. Yet, again at the very end, there is an intriguing section where Langdon is discussing with a priest the line from William Blake that forms the password to Kirsch's computer, the search for which plays a prominent role in the plot-line of the book: "The dark Religions are departed & sweet Science reigns."[17]

Langdon suggests to the priest that this could mean that science destroys the dark and bad religions but not the enlightened ones. There is truth in that. For science has indeed got rid of the "god of the gaps" type religions of the ancient Greeks, for instance, that stood in the way of the advance of science, but science has certainly not got rid of God the Creator and Upholder of the universe as revealed in the Judeo-Christian heritage, whose intelligent creation inspired the pioneer scientists in the first place.[18]

NOTES

1. Adam Paul Johnson et al., "The Miller Volcanic Spark Discharge Experiment," *Science* 322 (5900): 404 (November 2008), www.ncbi.nlm.nih.gov/pubmed /18927386.

2. Dan Brown, *Origin* (New York: Doubleday, 2017), 89.

3. Jeremy England, "Dan Brown Can't Cite Me to Disprove God," *Wall Street Journal*, 12 October 2017, www.wsj.com/articles/dan-brown-cant-cite-me-to -disprove-god-1507847369.

4. James Tour, "An Open Letter to My Colleagues," *Inference: International Review of Science* 3, no. 2 (August 2017), https://inference-review.com/article /an-open-letter-to-my-colleagues.

5. Tour, "Open Letter"; see also James Tour, "Animadversions of a Synthetic Chemist," *Inference: International Review of Science* 2, no. 2 (May 2016), https:// inference-review.com/article/animadversions-of-a-synthetic-chemist.

6. Cited by Clive Cookson, "Scientists Who Glimpsed God," *Financial Times*, 29 April 1995, 20.

7. C. S. Lewis, *Miracles: A Preliminary Study* (1947; repr., New York: Macmillan, 1978), 59.

8. Brown, *Origin*, 420 (italics original).

9. Lewis, *Miracles*, 106.

10. Brown, *Origin*, 421.

11. Michael Ruse, *Darwinism as Religion* (Oxford: Oxford University Press, 2016).

12. Brown, *Origin*, 435.

13. Brown, *Origin*, 436.

14. Donald Knuth, *Things a Computer Scientist Rarely Talks About* (Stanford, CA: CSLI Publications, 2001), 168.

15. "There Is a God, Leading Atheist Concludes: Philosopher Says Scientific Evidence Changed His Mind," *Associated Press*, 9 December 2004, www.nbcnews .com/id/6688917/ns/world_news/t/there-god-leading-atheist-concludes; see Antony Flew, *There Is a God* (New York: HarperOne, 2007). For more detail, see Stephen

Meyer, *Signature in the Cell* (New York: HarperOne, 2009), and my *God's Undertaker: Has Science Buried God?* (Oxford: Lion, 2009), 135–62.

16. Francis Collins, "Why This Scientist Believes in God," *CNN Commentary*, 6 April 2006, www.cnn.com/2007/US/04/03/collins.commentary/index.html; see Francis Collins, *The Language of God* (New York: Free Press, 2006).

17. William Blake, *The Four Zoas: Night the Ninth*, in *The Complete Poetry and Prose of William Blake*, ed. David Erdman (Berkeley: University of California Press, 1981), 407.

18. See my book *God's Undertaker*.

CHAPTER THREE

SECOND BIG QUESTION: WHERE ARE WE GOING?

It's tough to make predictions,
especially about the future.

Yogi Berra

Dan Brown's purported resolution of our first big question uses mathematical modelling and an AI system working on an immense database of information to make predictions about the evolution of a mixture of chemicals in the past. It is not hard, therefore, to guess how he will approach the second big question.

He proceeds this time to apply a similar methodology to extrapolate a simulation of human evolution into the future. The result that is revealed at the end of the book (spoiler alert, I fear) is that his AI system, working on another immense database consisting, in the main, of information gleaned from past information about bone fragments and changing environments over time, shows the eventual development of a new species. Rather than species, in a more exact taxonomy we should say a new kingdom, that, instead of branching as usual from an existing species, is a fusion of two "species," humans and AI.

He calls this new kingdom "Technium." It is a non-living species, by which he presumably means a non-biological species, although that is hard to square with his notion that it is a *fusion* of human biological life with technology. His projection shows that it eventually replaces the human race by 2050, and it does so by absorption! One is tempted to think that this is no more than entertaining science fiction. Indeed, it may turn out to be just that, yet it is only fair to say that not everyone is prepared to say it is science fiction.

For it is, apparently, no accident that Kirsch's name begins with K, since he seems to have been modelled on Ray Kurzweil, prolific inventor and Google's director of engineering. Kurzweil is the author of *The Singularity Is Near*, a book that unpacks his belief that within the foreseeable future, possibly as few as thirty years, AI robots will overtake humans in their intelligence and capabilities: "The nonbiological portion of our intelligence will predominate."[1]

Nick Bostrom of Oxford's Future of Life Institute calls this event the "intelligence explosion" in his book *Superintelligence*.[2] In the same vein, Ray Kurzweil says: "The 21st century will be different. The human species, along with the computational technology it created, will be able to solve age-old problems . . . and will be in a position to change the nature of mortality in a postbiological future."[3] This is the vision of AGI – artificial general intelligence. The fundamental idea here goes back to a deservedly famous quote from an article written in 1965 by statistician I. J. Good entitled "Speculations Concerning the First Ultraintelligent Machine":

Let an ultraintelligent machine be defined as a machine that can far surpass all the intellectual activities of any man however clever. Since the design of machines is one of these intellectual activities, an ultraintelligent machine could design even better machines; there would then unquestionably be an "intelligence explosion," and the intelligence of man would be left far behind. Thus the first ultraintelligent machine is the last invention that man need ever make.[4]

We should notice that we have now left the concept of undirected Darwinian evolution far behind in this scenario. The accelerating advances in the realm of technology, robots, and AI have all been due to human intelligent design. What Kurzweil predicts, therefore, involves artefacts designed by humans, in the sense that humans got the whole thing going until, in some scenarios, those artefacts possess more than human intelligence and take over their own subsequent development.

Dan Brown's AI expert, Kirsch, points out that, as we are all aware, to a certain extent, we have already started to merge with our own technology – we wear virtual reality glasses; we hold our mobile phones close to our ears; we have all kinds of high-quality headphones; and we are starting to embed computer chips into our brains, for instance, to cure deafness. We are also constructing more and more sophisticated prosthetic limbs, growing spare parts for our bodies, tinkering with our genetic structures, and exploring the possibilities and potential for genetic enhancement.

Kirsch's grand conclusion is: "New technologies like cybernetics, synthetic intelligence, cryonics, molecular engineering, and virtual reality will forever change what it means to be *human*. And I realize there are those of you who believe you, as *Homo sapiens*, are God's chosen species. I can understand that this news may feel like the end of the world to you. But I beg you, please believe me . . . the future is actually much *brighter* than you imagine."[5]

We are now firmly in the realm of AGI (artificial general intelligence) or, simply, general AI, that typically denotes attempts to construct a machine that can simulate equal or greater intelligence than a human being – in short, a superintelligence.

Related to that is the parallel quest to enhance human beings themselves in what is often called the transhumanism project. Nick Bostrom explains that transhumanism is: "the intellectual and cultural movement that affirms the possibility and desirability of fundamentally improving the human condition through applied reason, especially by developing and making widely available technologies to eliminate aging and to greatly enhance human intellectual, physical, and psychological capacities."[6]

Many people (including Bostrom) believe that the word *transhumanism* originated with atheist Julian Huxley (1887–1975): "'I believe in transhumanism': once there are enough people who can truly say that, the human species will be on the threshold of a new kind of existence, as different from ours as ours is from that of Peking man. It will at last be consciously fulfilling its real destiny."[7]

But Huxley was not the first. The origin of the word *transhuman* is not secular. Historically, it was first used, not by a scientist in connection with science, but regarding the resurrection of the body by Henry Francis Cary in his 1814 translation of Dante's *Paradiso*. It occurs in a passage where Dante tries to imagine the resurrection of his own body: "Words may not tell of that transhuman change."[8]

Contemporary ideas surrounding transhumanism are whole-brain emulation, cyborgs (= cybernetic organism), and in the hope that life extension will one day be realised, some people have paid for the freezing of their bodies and/or brains (cryonics).

We quoted Sir Martin Rees earlier. The wider context of what he said is:

> We should be mindful of an unprecedented kind of change that could emerge within a few decades. Human beings themselves – their mentality and their physique – may become malleable through the deployment of genetic modification and cyborg technologies. This is a game changer. When we admire the literature and artefacts that have survived from antiquity, we feel an affinity, across a time gulf of thousands of years, with those ancient artists and their civilisations. But we can have zero confidence that the dominant intelligences a few centuries hence will have any emotional resonance with us – even though they may have an algorithmic understanding of how we behaved.[9]

It is this kind of transhumanist AGI prediction that makes some people anxious, even filled with Orwellian alarm, at the possibility that robots will, perhaps sooner than we might imagine, become more intelligent than humans, take over our jobs, and, even worse, eventually rebel against humans and

47

destroy them as inferiors of no further value – *1984* with a vengeance. For instance, Elon Musk thinks that AI is "summoning the demon."[10] In 2015, together with more than 8,000 people, including Stephen Hawking and Noam Chomsky, he signed an open letter warning against potential "pitfalls" of AI development. In connection with this open letter, the paper "Research Priorities for Robust and Beneficial Artificial Intelligence" by Stuart Russell, Daniel Dewey, and Max Tegmark concludes:

> In summary, success in the quest for artificial intelligence has the potential to bring unprecedented benefits to humanity, and it is therefore worthwhile to research how to maximize these benefits while avoiding potential pitfalls. The research agenda outlined in this paper, and the concerns that motivate it, have been called anti-AI, but we vigorously contest this characterization. It seems self-evident that the growing capabilities of AI are leading to an increased potential for impact on human society. It is the duty of AI researchers to ensure that the future impact is beneficial. We believe that this is possible, and hope that this research agenda provides a helpful step in the right direction.[11]

In his book *Brief Answers to the Big Questions*, published posthumously, Hawking repeats his concern:

> While primitive forms of artificial intelligence developed so far have proved very useful, I fear the consequences of creating something that can match or surpass humans . . . Humans, who are limited by slow biological evolution, couldn't compete and would be superseded. And in the

future AI could develop a will of its own, a will that is in conflict with ours ... The real risk with AI isn't malice but competence. A super-intelligent AI will be extremely good at accomplishing its goals, and if those goals aren't aligned with ours we're in trouble.[12]

Shades of George Orwell.

Others are less cautious and take the view that all such developments are to be welcomed as they have already led to many obvious benefits and will keep doing so at increasing speed, thus building a world that is immeasurably better for all. Among them are Bill Gates and Mark Zuckerberg.

However, some neuroscientists are very sceptical. Jean Mariani, who directs an institute researching longevity, and Danièle Tritsch, former co-director of a neuroscience research laboratory, write:

Let's face it, all of this is pure fantasy ... Ageing is unavoidable, even if there is good reason to hope that it will be accompanied by improved health ... While progress over the last 50 years has brought a far better understanding of the brain, it has had little therapeutic impact. All of the predictions trumpeted by the transhumanists are at the very least, false ... Many have suggested that human intelligence may soon be outstripped by artificial intelligence. But this fear betrays a deep misunderstanding of what human intelligence really is.[13]

Opinion, therefore, is deeply divided. In any case, we must ask what these developments might mean for our understanding of who we are and what we might become.

In this connection, as hinted above, the quest for AGI needs to be distinguished from the parallel quest to upgrade human beings, although there is inevitably some overlap. We may think of one of the objectives of AGI as decoupling life from biology and constructing artificial life based on some other substrate, probably silicon.

Upgrading humans, on the other hand, means starting with human life as it is now and enhancing it, modifying it, fitting it with implanted technology (some of which may involve AGI) so that a superintelligent composite like Technium or *Homo deus* is produced. It is to be noted that, in Dan Brown's fictional scenario, a narrow AI system was used to *predict* the merging of humans with technology, but AI did not *perform* the upgrading itself. His AI genius had no means to do that. Nor, indeed, is there much evidence that anyone else has it either, or will ever have it.

We should note in passing that the terminology in this area can be somewhat fluid, for which reason some people prefer the term *IA* (intelligence augmentation) rather than the term *AI*. It is also useful to differentiate between several different project objectives and first to ask: what are our starting materials? When people talk of *making* artificial life, they generally mean this kind of construction from inorganic materials like steel, glass, copper, or silicon from scratch. After all, humans can make human life in a sense by in vitro fertilisation, but there they are starting with living cells which are real and not artificial life. Upgrading humanity means starting with human life and modifying it organically and/or adding technology to it so that what is eventually produced is composite and therefore only partly artificial.

To sum up: in the view of some people, AGI is what might eventually be done by human intelligence to produce artificial life and possibly consciousness; *upgrading humanity* is what can be done with human biological life to enhance it. Both are aimed at producing a superhuman superintelligence. Whether they will ever do so is another matter entirely and remains to be seen.

Such scenarios raise several obvious questions.

1. What does it mean to be human?
2. In what sense will technology change what it means to be human?
3. What are the ethical norms that should be applied to AI developments?
4. Is "rights" a meaningful category when applied to AGI?
5. How will technological advances affect the way in which people, believers or unbelievers, think of God?
6. Is the future really "much brighter than you imagine"?

NOTES

1. Ray Kurzweil, *The Singularity Is Near* (New York: Penguin, 2005), 201.

2. Nick Bostrom, *Superintelligence: Paths, Dangers, Strategies* (Oxford: Oxford University Press, 2014), 62.

3. Cited in Meghan O'Gieblyn, "God in the Machine: My Strange Journey into Transhumanism," *The Guardian*, 18 April 2017, www.theguardian.com/technology /2017/apr/18/god-in-the-machine-my-strange-journey-into-transhumanism.

4. I. J. Good, "Speculations Concerning the First Ultraintelligent Machine," in *Advances in Computers*, vol. 6, ed. F. L. Alt and M. Rubinoff (New York: Academic Press, 1965), 33. The importance of the idea of the singularity is examined in David J. Chalmers, "The Singularity: A Philosophical Analysis," *Journal of Consciousness Studies* 17:7–65 (2010), http://consc.net/papers/singularity.pdf.

5. Dan Brown, *Origin* (New York: Doubleday, 2017), 411, italics original.

6. Nick Bostrom, "The Transhumanist FAQ: A General Introduction," in *Transhumanism and the Body: The World Religions Speak*, ed. Calvin Mercer and Derek F. Maher (New York: Palgrave Macmillan, 2014), 1, www.nickbostrom.com/views/transhumanist.pdf.

7. Julian Huxley, *New Bottles for New Wine* (London: Chatto & Windus, 1957), 17.

8. Dante Alighieri, *The Vision; or Hell, Purgatory, and Paradise*, vol. 3 (London: Taylor and Hessey, 1819), 8.

9. Martin Rees, *On the Future* (Princeton, NJ: Princeton University Press, 2018), 7.

10. Quoted in Matt McFarland, "Elon Musk: 'With Artificial Intelligence We Are Summoning the Demon,'" *Washington Post*, 24 October 2014.

11. Stuart Russell, Daniel Dewey, and Max Tegmark, "Research Priorities for Robust and Beneficial Artificial Intelligence," *AI Magazine* (Winter 2015), https://futureoflife.org/data/documents/research_priorities.pdf.

12. Stephen Hawking, *Brief Answers to the Big Questions* (London: Murray, 2018), 186, 188.

13. Jean Mariani and Danièle Tritsch, "Is Transhumanism a Sham?" *CNRS News*, 9 June 2018, https://news.cnrs.fr/opinions/is-transhumanism-a-sham.

CHAPTER FOUR

NARROW ARTIFICIAL INTELLIGENCE: THE FUTURE IS BRIGHT?

The questions raised at the end of the previous chapter are of considerable general interest. In order to address them, we shall have to think carefully about what technologies we are talking about, what their positive benefits are, whether there are any risks associated with them, and whether they raise ethical problems.

As I warned before, one of the dangers of introducing futuristic and speculative scenarios in which humans are gradually merged with technology is that the impression is given that AI is only concerned with speculative and scary ideas whose implementation is just around the corner. That is not so. One of the winners of the 2018 Turing Prize, Yann LeCun, Chief AI Scientist at Facebook, says: "Whether we'll be able to use new methods to create human-level intelligence, well, there's probably another 50 mountains to climb, including ones we can't even see yet. We've only climbed the first mountain. Maybe the second."[1] We therefore need carefully to separate reality from hype and get our feet back onto the ground by thinking some more about narrow AI and what it has actually achieved.

It is worth pointing out that, historically, AI has had a bumpy ride. When researchers coined the term *AI* in 1956, they imagined that one summer's work by a small team would show that every feature of learning and intelligence could be conducted by a machine! Those early expectations were unrealistic, as more than sixty years later, their question is still unanswered. For a time, AI fell into disfavour, but with the availability of greatly enhanced computing power, it is now riding high. The UK is planning to invest in educating 1,000 PhDs in AI with a £1.3 billion fund set up in 2018. According to the *Times Higher Education*, between 2011 and 2015 China published 41,000 articles on AI, nearly twice as many as the US with 25,500 – way ahead of the rest.[2] In 2018, MIT announced the single largest investment in computing and AI by an American academic institution: $1 billion.[3] Also, China is investing many billions of dollars in AI research, and other countries are following suit in a battle for world dominance.[4]

Of course, experience tells us that most technological advances are likely to have both an upside and a downside. A knife can be used for surgery or as a murder weapon; a car can be used to take you to work or as a getaway vehicle after a crime. It is the same with AI. There are many valuable positive developments, and there are some very alarming negative aspects that demand close ethical attention.

Here are some ways in which AI is already proving of value.

Digital assistants. We have seen that AI is the capability of a computer system to use mathematical algorithms to perform a task or tasks that normally require human intelligence and is the technology that enables digital assistants like Alexa and Siri to answer our spoken questions, give recommendations for restaurants and entertainment, book travel and holidays, control the smart devices in our homes, and suggest things we might like to buy based on our past purchases – a list that is being added to daily. In fact, some digital assistants are being "trained" in advanced speech recognition so as to give early warning of possibly self-harming or even suicidal tendencies in their users. Scientists at Brown University are working with the toy manufacturer Hasbro to develop a robotic companion cat that can remind its owners when to take their medication and can track down their eyeglasses when they drop them.

Medicine. AI is being used in the development of new drugs, in the automation of medical treatments such as remote robotic operations, and as an aid to increase the efficiency of health provision. This is particularly true of the field of diagnostics. It is thought that by the end of 2019, at least half of leading healthcare systems will have adopted some form of AI. Before clinicians can harness the power of AI to identify conditions in images such as X-rays, they have to "teach" the algorithms what to look for. Engineers at the University of Toronto Faculty of Applied Science & Engineering have designed a new approach using machine learning to create computer-generated X-rays to augment AI training sets. They compared the accuracy of their augmented dataset to the original dataset when fed through their AI system and found that classification accuracy improved by 20 per cent for common conditions. For some rare conditions, accuracy improved up to about 40 per cent, and because the synthesized X-rays are not from real individuals, the dataset can be readily available to researchers outside the hospital premises without violating privacy concerns. Lead researcher Dr. Shahrokh Valaee says: "It's exciting because we've been able to overcome a hurdle in applying artificial intelligence to medicine by showing that these augmented datasets help to improve classification accuracy . . . Deep learning only works if the volume of training data is large enough and this is one way to ensure we have neural networks that can classify images with high precision."[5]

Another example of this kind of development is an AI system that can detect diabetic retinopathy, a condition caused by damage to the blood vessels of the light-sensitive tissue at the back of the eye and can lead to blindness. Deep learning AI matched or exceeded the performance of experts in identifying and grading the severity of the conditions. Interestingly, the software was not explicitly programmed to recognise features from images that might indicate the disease. It simply looked at thousands of healthy and diseased eyes and figured out for itself how to spot the condition. The number of potentially beneficial applications of systems like this seems essentially unlimited, and new ones are appearing every day.

Scientists in the University of Hong Kong have designed the first neurosurgical robotic system capable of performing bilateral stereotactic neurosurgery inside an MRI scanner. This is one of the treatments for a variety of movement and neuropsychiatric disorders, such as Parkinson's disease, essential tremor, and major depression. It involves a technique that can locate targets of surgical interest using an external positioning system, which is widely applied in brain biopsy, tumour ablation, drug delivery, as well as deep brain stimulation. Parkinson's disease alone is the second most common disease of the nervous system after Alzheimer's disease and is projected to affect more than 8.7 million people worldwide by 2030. As such, any improvement to this surgery would benefit a large population.[6]

The National Health Service (NHS) in the UK expects to be a world leader in AI and machine learning in five years' time: "Exploiting the boom in AI technology will help to meet the NHS Long Term Plan's target of making up to 30 million outpatient appointments unnecessary, saving over £1 billion in what would have been increasing outpatient visits which can then be reinvested in front line care, saving patients unnecessary journeys to hospitals."[7] The chief executive of NHS England has said: "Health providers will be paid to substitute clinicians with machines as the NHS embraces artificial intelligence to improve patient outcomes and deliver savings."[8]

However, even in the area of medicine, there could be a downside. For instance, a report into AI by the Academy of Medical Royal Colleges in the UK warns that the rise of health apps could eventually mean that medical services would be overwhelmed by the worried well whose AI-enabled smartphones or fitness attachments had erroneously told them they needed medical attention.[9]

I wish to end this section, however, on a positive note by referring to Rosalind Picard and her team at MIT and the company Empatica. They have created the first machine learning system that can recognise seizures using a smartwatch that is FDA-approved and on the market in the USA and EU.[10] The watch runs in connection with an AI algorithm that looks for real-time patterns of movements and electrical changes in the patient's skin that indicate a likely seizure. When such patterns are detected, it alerts the wearer (giving him or her a chance to cancel a possible false detection), and if it is not cancelled quickly, then the AI summons a caregiver for help. It can also let the caregiver know where the person in need of help is. It can do all of this continuously without requiring the wearer to do anything other than keep the smartwatch and mobile phone charged.

It is important to realise that when the most dangerous type of seizure strikes, it renders its victim unconscious and hence unable to call for help; the most dangerous period of time is in minutes after it appears the seizure has ended, when in fact activity deep in the brain can change and turn off respiration, which has a good chance of being restarted if a person arrives to provide first-aid. This smartwatch AI system has already been credited with summoning human help to save lives and has the potential over time to significantly reduce the number of deaths in epilepsy (which currently takes more lives every year than house fires or sudden infant death syndrome).

Picard's Affective Computing lab at MIT has also been developing AI/machine learning to help people see if they are sliding into depression, long before they would need a diagnosis (so that hopefully they could take measures to prevent getting depressed).[11] The examples in the referenced article are all narrow AI, targeted at helping prevent illness, and "knowing" nothing, just finding patterns that are probabilistically associated with potential needs. Such data collection, of course, raises the ethical question of the potentiality of medical data falling into the wrong hands.

Autonomous vehicles. A great deal of research effort is being poured into the design and development of self-driving vehicles. The aim is to make the roads safer by having AI systems that make faster and better decisions than human drivers. Chinese researchers at the University of Tsinghua have managed to combine two different types of AI systems – a traditional one that recognises objects and hazards and one modelled on biology that can control balance and voice – in order to construct a riderless bicycle that responds to commands.[12]

Autonomous vehicles give rise to a whole new set of ethical issues: how, for instance, should the system be programmed to ensure that the vehicle will avoid accidents to people and property, especially if it has to choose between people and objects it is likely to hit through no fault of its own. Systems have to have values built in, and someone has to decide what those values are. This issue is the tip of an iceberg in AI, since all are agreed that the technology is developing far faster than the ethics to cope with it.

Language translators. Since childhood I have been interested in languages and managed to learn German to a high enough level to be able to lecture in it. I used to write my lectures in German, laboriously looking up the words that were not yet part of my active vocabulary, so that the whole process took up a lot of time. Now all I need to do is write the lecture in English, feed it into Google Translate, and within a few seconds I have a German translation that I can read through, make a few corrections, and I am ready to go. This is a phenomenally useful development. There are many variants of the technology: speech translation, speech-to-text, text-to-speech – with or without translation.

Advertising. AI is used in internet advertising by companies like Amazon, Alphabet (which owns Google), or China's

Alibaba and Baidu to suggest articles you might like to purchase based on your, and other people's, online activity. For instance, yesterday I had a look at flights online, and today I received a message saying: "We couldn't help noticing that you were considering a flight to X. Why not book now." Such tracking algorithms are pursuing us all the time.

Not only that, but AI systems have been developed to construct the adverts themselves. *The Times* reported that the largest bank in the United States – JPMorgan Chase – signed a deal with Persado, a marketing company that uses AI to create adverts.[13] They ran a test that showed that the use of AI led to about four and a half times more hits on a site advertising mortgages and credit cards.

Industry. Carnegie Mellon University announced in April 2018 that they have developed an AI algorithm that will automate not only the carrying out of experiments to find the best high-capacity car battery, but also the planning and decision-making stages. Another example is a robotic "flying scarecrow" using an AI system that has been developed to keep flocks of birds away from airports.

This list, which is getting longer every day, should be enough to demonstrate that research into AI has brought about considerable achievements. It is worth, however, making sure that we do not get carried away. On 14 November 2018, Stephen Shankland reported in CNET that the vice president of AI for Google's iCloud had said the previous day that "AI is still very, very stupid. It is really good at doing certain things which our brains can't handle but it is not something we could press to do general-purpose reasoning like analogies or creative thinking or jumping outside the box."[14] Similarly, *Forbes* contributor Kalev Leetaru reminds us:

At the end of the day the deep learning systems are less "AI" than [they are] fancy pattern extractors. Like any machine learning system, they are able to blindly identify the underlying patterns in their training data and apply those patterns as-is to future data. They cannot reason about their input data or generalize to higher order abstractions that would allow them to more completely and robustly understand their data. In short, while they can perform impressive feats, deep learning systems are still extraordinarily limited, with brittleness that can manifest in highly unexpected ways.

After all, the "AI" of today's deep learning revolution is still just machine learning, not magic.[15]

Nevertheless, many people would agree with the optimistic stance of Astronomer Royal Sir Martin Rees, who says: "Our lives, our health and our environment can benefit still more from further progress in biotech, cybertech, robotics, and AI. To that extent, I am a techno-optimist." Rees continues: "But there is a potential downside. These advances expose our interconnected world to ever new vulnerabilities."[16] It is to that potential downside that we must now turn.

NOTES

1. Quoted in James Vincent, "'Godfathers of AI' Honored with Turing Award, the Nobel Prize of Computing," *The Verge* 27 (March 2019), www.theverge.com/2019/3/27/18280665/ai-godfathers-turing-award-2018-yoshua-bengio-geoffrey-hinton-yann-lecun.

2. Cited in Bruno Jacobsen, "5 Countries Leading the Way in AI," Futures Platform, 8 January 2018, www.futuresplatform.com/blog/5-countries-leading-way-ai-artificial-intelligence-machine-learning.

3. See "MIT Reshapes Itself to Shape the Future," *MIT News*, 15 October

2018, http://news.mit.edu/2018/mit-reshapes-itself-stephen-schwarzman-college -of-computing-1015.

4. See Thomas Davenport, "China Is Catching Up to the US on Artificial Intelligence Research," *The Conversation*, 27 February 2019, https://theconversation .com/china-is-catching-up-to-the-us-on-artificial-intelligence-research-112119.

5. University of Toronto Faculty of Applied Science & Engineering, "Training Artificial Intelligence with Artificial X-rays," *ScienceDaily*, 6 July 2018, www .sciencedaily.com/releases/2018/07/180706150816.htm.

6. See The University of Hong Kong, "World's First Intra-operative MRI-Guided Robot for Bilateral Stereotactic Neurosurgery," *ScienceDaily*, 19 June 2018, www .sciencedaily.com/releases/2018/06/180619122517.htm.

7. "NHS Aims to Be a World Leader in Artificial Intelligence and Machine Learning within 5 Years," *NHS News*, 5 June 2019, www.longtermplan.nhs.uk/nhs-aims- to-be-a-world-leader-in-artificial-intelligence-and-machine-learning-within-5-years.

8. Philip Aldrick, "Hospitals to Get Extra Cash for Using Robots and AI to Replace Humans," *The Times*, 6 June 2019, www.thetimes.co.uk/article /hospitals-robots-ai-replace-humans-nhs-simon-stevens-8dhztxtlc.

9. See Kat Lay, "Patients Fretting about Fitbit Data Could Overwhelm Doctors," *The Times*, 28 January 2019, www.thetimes.co.uk/article/patients-fretting -about-fitbit-data-could-overwhelm-doctors-fkl5mwzbd.

10. "Embrace by Empatica Is the World's First Smart Watch to Be Cleared by FDA for Use in Neurology," *PR Newswire*, 5 February 2018, www.prnewswire.com /news-releases/embrace-by-empatica-is-the-worlds-first-smart-watch-to-be-cleared -by-fda-for-use-in-neurology-300593398.html.

11. Matt Kaplan, "Happy with a 20% Chance of Sadness," *Nature* 563 (2018), 20–22, www.nature.com/articles/d41586-018-07181-8.

12. See Tom Whipple, "Riderless Bike Can Balance and Steer Itself," *The Times*, 1 August 2019, www.thetimes.co.uk/article/riderless-bike-can-balance-and -steer-itself-97r5w6wpn.

13. See Tom Knowles, "Mad Men versus Machines as Robots Write Ad Slogans," *The Times*, 1 August 2019, www.thetimes.co.uk/article/mad-men-versus -machines-as-robots-write-ad-slogans-mf7ggmff2.

14. Stephen Shankland, "'AI Is Very, Very Stupid,' Says Google's AI Leader, At Least Compared to Humans," *CNET*, 14 November 2018, www.cnet.com/news /ai-is-very-stupid-says-google-ai-leader-compared-to-humans.

15. Kalev Leetaru, "Today's Deep Learning 'AI' Is Machine Learning Not Magic," *Forbes*, 14 November 2018, www.forbes.com/sites/kalevleetaru/2018/11/14 /todays-deep-learning-ai-is-machine-learning-not-magic.

16. Martin Rees, *On the Future* (Princeton, NJ: Princeton University Press, 2018), 5.

CHAPTER FIVE

NARROW AI: PERHAPS THE FUTURE IS NOT SO BRIGHT AFTER ALL?

Job recruitment. One increasing application of AI that initially seems positive is in assisting large corporations with hiring new employees. For instance, a technology venture called HireVue has developed a platform that simplifies the job interviewing process. The most common use of that is an interview where a set of questions is created. Candidates respond on video, and then artificial intelligence algorithms are used to evaluate the candidate's performance. HireVue then analyses the interview and predicts their performance. The system looks at 25,000 different features and complex relationships between them. It might see things that a human observer cannot see.

The Guardian reported on Sunday, 4 March 2018:

After 86 unsuccessful job applications in two years – including several HireVue screenings – Deborah Caldeira is thoroughly disillusioned with automated systems. Without a person across the table, there's "no real conversation or exchange," and it's difficult to know "exactly what the robot is looking for," says Caldeira, who has a master's degree from the London School of Economics.

Despite her qualifications, she found herself questioning every movement as she sat at home alone performing for a computer. "It makes us feel that we're not worthwhile, as the company couldn't even assign a person for a few minutes. The whole thing is becoming less human," she says.[1]

Threat of job losses. Getting a job is one thing; losing it is another, and a deepening concern on the part of many people is whether their jobs are themselves at risk from developments in robotics and (narrow) AI. It is of course true that every revolution in industry has the effect of closing down some jobs but then, eventually, creating new ones. Think, for example, of the consequences of the invention of the wheelbarrow, the steam engine, or the electric motor and automobile.

Earlier industrial revolutions have seen machines replacing humans doing manual things. The AI revolution will increasingly see machines replacing humans doing thinking things at all levels. For instance, it has been estimated that some 85 per cent of customer interactions will be managed by AI by 2020, and the Serious Fraud Office in the UK is already using an AI system instead of barristers to sift through case documents in order to identify relevant evidence.

MIT Technology Review reported in early 2017: "At its height back in 2000, the U.S. cash equities trading desk at Goldman Sachs's New York headquarters employed 600 traders . . . Today there are just two equity traders left. Automated trading programs have taken over the rest of the work, supported by 200 computer engineers."[2] Of course, the fact that it is technically possible to replace a worker with a robot does not mean that it makes economic sense to do so. Predictions as to the numbers of jobs at risk vary greatly according to who is doing the forecasting. In 2016, a team led by Katja Grace from the Future of Humanity Institute at the University of Oxford surveyed the views of 352 academics and industry experts in machine learning. Here are some of the conclusions of that survey:

> In the next ten years, we should have A.I. do better than humans in translating languages (by 2024), writing high-school-level essays (by 2026), writing top 40 songs (by 2028) and driving trucks. And while the consensus may be that driving trucks may come by 2027, it's easy to predict that this could happen even sooner . . .
>
> A chore that would take less time – folding laundry should be a breeze for A.I. by 2022 . . . We should get A.I.-driven machines in retail by 2031. By 2049, A.I. should be writing *New York Times* bestsellers and performing surgeries by 2053.
>
> Overall, A.I. should be better than humans at pretty much everything in about 45 years.[3]

The survey also indicated that all human jobs would be automated within the next 125 years.

The Bank of England's chief economist, Andy Haldane, speaks of a "hollowing out of the jobs market" caused by technological advance which "left a lot of people ... struggling to make a living. That heightened social tensions, it heightened financial tensions, it led to a rise in inequality." Haldane says that there is "a dark side" to technological revolutions, and "we will need even greater numbers of new jobs to be created in the future, if we are not to suffer this longer-term feature called technological unemployment."[4]

One report by PwC predicted that about 7 million jobs could be displaced by 2020 but 7.2 million could be created.[5] The fact is that we just do not know with any precision how jobs will be affected, but that they will be affected is clear – they already are.

Scientist Sir Martin Rees agrees that robots may take over many jobs but suggests that they will never be any good at caring, an activity that lies at the heart of what it means to be human. However, this is not quite true. Granted that robots do not care in the same way as humans care, yet Dr. Rosalind Picard's group at MIT has published studies about the creation of robotic text-based chat and conversational agents that appeared to people as if they really do care to the extent that those interacting responded to them by acting in ways that showed the technology was achieving real success. Picard comments:

> This, like all AI to date, works only in very narrow contexts, but also it is very good in those contexts. People perceive the AIs that use empathetic language as more "caring" than AIs that simply use friendly or social language or that just provide information. This work has been continued by people building social robots and has been deployed in products – e.g., by Cory Kidd of Catalia Health.[6]

2084 – BIG BROTHER MEETS BIG DATA

One of the major Orwellian aspects of AI is that certain forms of it present a serious threat to individual and corporate privacy. AI tracker programs are geared to harvesting as much data as possible that you generate about yourself – your lifestyle, habits, where you go, what you buy, people you communicate with, books you read, jobs you do, political and social activities, your personal opinions – a list that is being added to all the time. Mark Zuckerberg once boasted that Facebook would know every book, film, and song a person had ever consumed and that its predictive models would tell you what bar to go to when you arrive in a strange city, where the bartender would have your favourite drink waiting for you.[7] Some of this we find helpful, but there is more than one side to it. Data that is harvested from us can be used not only to inform us but to control us.

For obvious reasons, criminals also wish to get their hands on this data. At the time of writing, I learned that my credit card details had been hacked from a well-known company to whom I entrusted them. As a result, I had to cancel the card and order another one in order to avoid being the victim of financial crime.

We already live in a world where around 2.5 billion of us (voluntarily, be it noted) wear a sophisticated personal tracker in the shape of a smartphone, and almost the same number are networked on Facebook. The big ethical questions are obvious: Who controls such projects and who owns the data they generate?

Surveillance Capitalism

The harvesting of data has become an immensely profitable business that has subtle and often hidden ramifications. This issue is the subject of an impressive recent book, *The Age of Surveillance Capitalism* by Harvard Professor Shoshana Zuboff. It is subtitled: *The Fight for a Human Future at the New Frontier of Power.*[8] Her thesis is that we are moving into what she defines at the beginning of her book as a new kind of economic order that collects the big data that we generate and exploits it as raw material for the purpose of making money in ways that are less than obvious to most people. These activities will, of course, intensify the risk of the kind of surveillance society that we shall discuss in the next section, and the two together will threaten the stability and freedoms that are currently enjoyed in at least some parts of the world.

Zuboff, whose voice is already being regarded as one that should not be ignored, also makes the important point that surveillance capitalism is a logical consequence of the technologies that are being developed.[9] At a more popular level, Libby Purves comments in *the Times* of 29 July 2019 on the prevalence of digital assistants like Siri and Alexa: "Novelty blurs the oddity of paying to live with a vigilant inhuman spy linked to an all-too-human corporate profit centre thousands of miles away . . . To welcome an ill-regulated corporate eavesdropper into your house is a dumb, reckless bit of self-bugging."[10] Yet millions, maybe soon billions, of us do it!

Surveillance Communism

Just as one downside of information harvesting is surveillance capitalism, another might be reasonably called surveillance communism. In March 2018, the Future of Humanity Institute at the University of Oxford published a report on the development of AI in China, where, it is said, $197 billion was spent on domestic security in 2017 and where they expect to install more than 400 million CCTV cameras by 2020. Some of what George Orwell envisaged for 1984 is already with us, so what it will be like by 2084 is anybody's guess, although the underlying trend is clear – China is already using AI in order to achieve social control.[11]

They are gradually rolling out a social credit system in order to check on the reliability and trustworthiness of citizens. The system consists in starting each citizen with the award of 300 social credit points that can be added to by "good" (i.e., government-approved) behaviour – like using public transport, keeping fit, reporting on someone you have seen with large amounts of foreign currency. As your points accumulate, you are granted more and more perks – access to a wider range of jobs, mortgage opportunities, school placements for children, goods, travel possibilities, etc.

If you behave in ways thought "anti-social," like associating with people regarded "unsafe" by the government, coming into conflict with the police, or overindulging in alcohol, you will lose points, and that will eventually result in penalties – limited access to the job and housing market, restrictions on travel or even on the range of restaurants you can visit, etc. You might even end up being denounced as a "discredited person" on a public television screen as you walk past it.

Much of this control is exercised by the use of advanced AI facial recognition techniques working on a vast database of images channelled into a central computing centre from what will soon be millions of CCTV cameras.[12]

The Times reported that some Chinese companies are fitting their employees with headgear that conceals technology that can read the wearer's brainwaves and send the data to computers that, in turn, use AI to check for emotions such as depression, anxiety, or anger.[13] Six months later, we learned that China plans to implement the social credit programme for all of the almost 22 million citizens of Beijing. *The Telegraph* reported that the Chinese government has stated that "the points system will improve the city's business environment by preventing people with low 'integrity' from accessing the city's public services and travel network. People with a low credit score could also find it difficult to start a business or find work."[14] Channel News Asia reported in March that nine million people had already been blocked from buying tickets for domestic flights and three million from obtaining business-class train tickets.[15]

It is not hard to see that these plans represent a massive hacking of human beings and are taking the world a rather scary step towards the perfection of a (potentially global) dictatorship, the setting up of an "authoritarian dream world" whose ideology could spread around the world like a virus and whose legitimacy is secured by the most comprehensive and powerful state surveillance apparatus in history. China's Police Cloud System is built to monitor seven categories of people, including those who "undermine stability."[16]

There would now appear to be a huge hidden ethical problem here. It has to do with the assumption that the AI facial recognition algorithms and the wearable emotion-detection technology give correct readings of the emotions and attitudes they are meant to detect. But there is increasing scientific evidence that this may be far from the case, at least in the case of facial recognition.

The Times of 29 July 2019 reports on a two-year analysis of more than 1,000 studies of the relationship between facial movements and emotions. The researchers did not find support for stereotypical facial expressions as predictive of feelings.[17] The conclusion stated by University Distinguished Professor of Psychology Lisa Feldman Barrett of Northeastern University in Massachusetts was this: "It is not possible to confidently infer happiness from a smile, anger from a scowl, or sadness from a frown."[18] Yet many major providers of security technologies think otherwise. The room for mistakes leading to tragic injustices for targeted individuals and groups is obvious. It seems that little is being done about it, even though such possibly flawed technologies are being rolled out, particularly in China.

In a more recent Human Rights Watch report, their senior China researcher, Maya Wang, said: "The Chinese government is monitoring every aspect of people's lives in Xinjiang, picking out those it mistrusts and subjecting them to extra scrutiny."[19]

Xinjiang is a region of western China that is home to ten million Uighur people, who are predominantly Muslim, and an increasing number of Han Chinese, who have been encouraged to settle there. The Chinese can move around without difficulty, but the Uighur population is now subject to the most intense surveillance that the world has ever seen to the extent that the capital city of Urumqi has been described as a "digital fortress." There are cameras every few metres down every street and alleyway. There are small police stations every few hundred yards, where passing Uighurs must hand in their smartphones to have them electronically read and all the information contained on them transferred to the central monitoring system to be processed by AI. A recent clandestine TV documentary made for ITV showed pictures of QR codes pasted on the doors of houses to be read by police scanners so that they would know who was supposed to be in the house and could then check.[20]

What is even more disturbing is the setting up of so-called "re-education centres" that together house up to a million Uighurs, who are sent there as a result of what is revealed by the surveillance apparatus, even though, as we have seen, the technology may be flawed. Many families have been split up – husbands taken from their wives and children taken from their parents. These "re-education centres" – prisons, really – appear to be devoted to the elimination of Uighur culture, turning their inmates into loyal Chinese citizens.[21] They represent an extreme violation of human rights – indeed, one commentator said that human rights for the Uighur population were non-existent.

Ms. Wang's report went on to say: "This is not just about Xinjiang or even China – it's about the world beyond and whether we human beings can continue to have freedom in a world of connected devices." She added: "It's a wake-up call, not just about China but about every one of us."[22]

Indeed so. For it is fairly obvious that most of the ingredients of such a social credit surveillance programme already exist in the West, though, as yet, in a non-centralised form. Last year, *The Times* revealed that a Chinese company had sold 1.2 million CCTV cameras to the UK, some of which can see in the dark, recognise number plates, and count the people entering and leaving buildings.[23] We all live in an age of corporate mass algorithmic surveillance. Trading freedom for security is in the air – an Orwellian dystopia with a vengeance. Remember the two-way televisions called "telescreens"? These developments recall the dystopian police state called One State, built almost entirely of glass to facilitate surveillance, that featured in one of the earliest books that inspired many subsequent dystopian novels, including *Brave New World* and, possibly, *1984*. I am referring to the 1921 science fiction novel *We* by Russian author Yevgeny Zamyatin.

At the moment in the West, many of the surveillance tools are (still) in private hands, although that seems to be changing. For instance, in 2015, France introduced the International Electronic Communications Law; in 2016, the UK introduced the Investigatory Powers Act, and Germany introduced the Communications Gathering Intelligence Act, all of which give increased surveillance powers to their security services.

Credit-scoring firms are increasingly dealing in indexes that bear no relation to a bank statement, such as individuals' social networks. Insurance companies fit cars with tracking transponders to keep tabs on their mileage. Some medical insurers give discounts to customers if they can see from their Fitbits that they have been exercising properly. Again, in *The Times* of 16 April 2018, Matt Ridley makes the point that "The handling of personal data by all too human intelligence has turned into the biggest ethical challenge of this brave new world."[24]

One well-known example is the deep concern over Facebook, which, as it turns out, has been storing records of its members' calls and texts, often without their knowing it, and allowing companies like Cambridge Analytica to access it on an unprecedented scale. This is the downside, some say the curse, of big data. The more that is known about how people behave in aggregate, the more we will be judged on the traces our choices and actions leave in cyberspace, and the more our future choices and actions will be shaped by these systems. They come closer and closer to the Chinese social credit programme. Ridley goes on to say: "Society must grapple with the dilemma of preserving people's privacy and ownership of their data while letting machine-learning algorithms harvest insights of value to everybody."

MILITARY USE OF AI: AUTONOMOUS WEAPONS

A Chatham House report says: "Both military and commercial robots will in the future incorporate 'artificial intelligence' (AI) that could make them capable of undertaking tasks and missions on their own. In the military context, this gives rise to a debate as to whether such robots should be allowed to execute such missions, especially if there is a possibility that any human life could be at stake."[25]

Tesla founder Elon Musk thinks that AI could trigger World War III, and Vladimir Putin has said that leadership in AI will be essential to global power in the twenty-first century. Michael Horowitz of the University of Pennsylvania sounds a cautious note:

The potential promise of AI, despite safety and reliability concerns, means leading militaries around the world will certainly see the risks of standing still. From data processing to swarming concepts to battlefield management, AI could help militaries operate faster and more accurately, while putting fewer humans at risk. Or not. The safety and reliability problems endemic to current machine learning and neural network methods mean that adversarial data, among other issues, will present a challenge to many military applications of AI . . . But given its breadth as a technology, as compared to specific technologies like directed energy, and the degree of commercial energy and investment in AI, it seems more likely that the age of artificial intelligence is likely to shape, at least to some extent, the future of militaries around the world.[26]

A report by Zachary Fryer-Biggs says that the Pentagon plans to spend $2 billion to put more AI into weaponry in order to compete more effectively with Russian and Chinese advances in military technology.[27] Apparently, however, commanders are concerned about relinquishing command to AI systems that would be tasked with identifying, searching out, and eliminating human targets. Google researchers who have been working on such AI systems have protested to such an extent that their part in the programme is being discontinued. Cited in the report, Horowitz comments: "There's a lot of concern about AI safety – [about] algorithms that are unable to adapt to complex reality and thus malfunction in unpredictable ways. It's one thing if what you're talking about is a Google search, but it's another thing if what you're talking about is a weapons system." In a keynote address at Stanford University in 2019, Bill Gates said that AI is like nuclear energy and nuclear weapons in being "both promising and dangerous."[28]

During the Cold War, a group of medical doctors called International Physicians for the Prevention of Nuclear War was awarded the Nobel Prize for Peace for warning against the apocalyptic use of nuclear weapons. Now that same group is impressing upon the world the need to act against the threat of killer robots and the danger of autonomous weapons falling into the hands of terrorists. A warning was given in March 2019 to a meeting of the United Nations: "AI technologies can also be used to create weapons of mass destruction unlike anything the world has seen before."[29]

It is clear that some very smart ethics needs to be developed to cope with this increasing threat before it is too late.

General ethical concerns regarding AI have led to the formulation of the so-called Asilomar AI Principles developed at a conference in Asilomar, California, in 2017, which have been subscribed to by more than 1,000 AI research workers. Other endorsers include the late Stephen Hawking, Elon Musk, and Jaan Tallinn. Some of the ethical principles taken from the list are:

1) **Research Goal:** The goal of AI research should be to create not undirected intelligence, but beneficial intelligence . . .

6) **Safety:** AI systems should be safe and secure throughout their operational lifetime, and verifiably so where applicable and feasible . . .

10) **Value Alignment:** Highly autonomous AI systems should be designed so that their goals and behaviors can be assured to align with human values throughout their operation.

11) **Human Values:** AI systems should be designed and operated so as to be compatible with ideals of human dignity, rights, freedoms, and cultural diversity.

12) **Personal Privacy:** People should have the right to access, manage and control the data they generate, given AI systems' power to analyze and utilize that data.

13) **Liberty and Privacy:** The application of AI to personal data must not unreasonably curtail people's real or perceived liberty.

14) **Shared Benefit:** AI technologies should benefit and empower as many people as possible.

15) **Shared Prosperity:** The economic prosperity created by AI should be shared broadly, to benefit all of humanity.

16) **Human Control:** Humans should choose how and whether to delegate decisions to AI systems, to accomplish human-chosen objectives.

17) **Non-subversion:** The power conferred by control of highly advanced AI systems should respect and improve, rather than subvert, the social and civic processes on which the health of society depends.

18) **AI Arms Race:** An arms race in lethal autonomous weapons should be avoided.

Longer-term issues are, for example, represented by:

20) **Importance:** Advanced AI could represent a profound change in the history of life on Earth, and should be planned for and managed with commensurate care and resources . . .

22) **Recursive Self-Improvement:** AI systems designed to recursively self-improve or self-replicate in a manner that could lead to rapidly increasing quality or quantity must be subject to strict safety and control measures.

23) **Common Good:** Superintelligence should only be developed in the service of widely shared ethical ideals,

and for the benefit of all humanity rather than one state or organization.[30]

The main thrust to these principles is to ensure that research in AI is ethically structured in such a way that the resultant systems are safe, secure, and designed in alignment with commonly held human values so that they are beneficial to humanity and lead to the flourishing of as many people as possible. Attempts to use advanced AI to develop superintelligence should be constrained by widely shared ethical convictions so that they serve the good of all human beings rather than the narrow interests of a state or corporation.

A word of realistic caution is in order: as every compliance manager knows, it is one thing to have a mission statement and a list of ethical principles; it is another thing to get them owned in the hearts, minds, and behaviour of those people for whom they were designed. That may well be the greatest problem of all in attempting to avoid the advent before 2084 of the scary aspects of Orwell's *1984*.

At the opening in the Speaker's House, Westminster, of the UK's first Institute for Ethical Artificial Intelligence in Education in October 2018, Sir Anthony Seldon, Vice-Chancellor of the University of Buckingham, said:

We are sleepwalking into the biggest danger that young people have faced, eclipsing totally the risk of social media and other forms of digitalization. The Government is not stepping up to the mark, and the tech companies are eating them alive, making shamefully high profits, preaching platitudes while infantilising our young and exposing them to great dangers. AI could be a considerable boon if we get the ethical dimension right but with each passing month we are losing the battle.[31]

Is it inevitable that Big Data will lead to Big Brother? The historian Yuval Noah Harari thinks so: "Once Big Data systems know me better than I know myself, authority will shift from humans to algorithms. Big Data could then empower Big Brother."[32]

NOTES

1. Stephen Buranyi, "How to Persuade a Robot That You Should Get the Job," *The Guardian*, 4 March 2018, www.theguardian.com/technology/2018/mar/04/robots-screen-candidates-for-jobs-artificial-intelligence.

2. Nanette Byrnes, "As Goldman Embraces Automation, Even the Masters of the Universe Are Threatened," *MIT Technology Review*, 7 February 2017, www.technologyreview.com/s/603431/as-goldman-embraces-automation-even-the-masters-of-the-universe-are-threatened.

3. Paul Ratner, "Here's When Machines Will Take Your Job, as Predicted by A.I. Gurus," *Big Think*, 4 June 2017, https://bigthink.com/paul-ratner/heres-when-machines-will-take-your-job-predict-ai-gurus.

4. Lucy Hook, "Bank of England Chief Economist Warns over Risk of AI Jobs Threat," *Insurance Business*, 20 August 2018, www.insurancebusinessmag.com/us/risk-management/operational/bank-of-england-chief-economist-warns-over-risk-of-ai-jobs-threat-109206.aspx.

5. See Anmar Frangoul, "Artificial Intelligence Will Create More Jobs Than It Destroys? That's What PwC Says," *CNBC*, 17 July 2018, www.cnbc.com/2018/07/17/artificial-intelligence-to-create-more-jobs-than-it-destroys-pwc-says.html.

6. Private communication (used with permission); see also T. Bickmore and R. W. Picard, "Towards Caring Machines," Proceedings of CHI, April 2004, Vienna, Italy; and, for more detail, T. Bickmore and R. W. Picard, "Establishing and Maintaining Long-Term Human-Computer Relationships," *Transactions on Computer-Human Interaction* 12, no. 2 (June 2004): 293–327.

7. Cited in Ashlee Vance, "Facebook: The Making of 1 Billion Users," *Bloomberg*, 4 October 2012, www.bloomberg.com/news/articles/2012-10-04/facebook-the-making-of-1-billion-users.

8. Shoshana Zuboff, *The Age of Surveillance Capitalism: The Fight for a Human Future at the New Frontier of Power* (London: Profile, 2019).

9. Zuboff, *Age of Surveillance Capitalism*, 15.

10. Libby Purves, "Hey Siri, I'd Like You to Leave Me Alone Now," *The Times*, 29 July 2019, www.thetimes.co.uk/article/hey-siri-i-d-like-you-to-leave -me-alone-now-qz5dlt8q3.

11. See Anna Mitchell and Larry Diamond, "China's Surveillance State Should Scare Everyone," *The Atlantic*, 2 February 2018, www.theatlantic.com/international /archive/2018/02/china-surveillance/552203.

12. See Jeffrey Ding, "Deciphering China's AI Dream: The Context, Components, Capabilities, and Consequences of China's Strategy to Lead the World in AI," Future of Humanity Institute, University of Oxford (March 2018), www.fhi.ox.ac.uk/wp -content/uploads/Deciphering_Chinas_AI-Dream.pdf, 33–34; see also Oliver Moody, "Big Brother Is Watching Them. And We're Next," *The Times*, 31 March 2018, www .thetimes.co.uk/article/big-brother-is-watching-them-and-we-re-next-858902nbk.

13. Didi Tang, "Chinese Read Brainwaves to Check Up on Workforce," *The Times*, 9 May 2018, www.thetimes.co.uk/article/china-chinese-read-brainwaves -workforce-technology-mood-detection-zp67vv9vx.

14. Joseph Archer, "Beijing to Assign 'Personal Trustworthiness Points' for All Citizens by 2021," *The Telegraph*, 20 November 2018, www.telegraph.co.uk /technology/2018/11/20/beijing-assign-personal-trustworthiness-points-citizens-2021.

15. Cited in Alexandra Ma, "China Ranks Citizens with a Social Credit System – Here's What You Can Do Wrong and How You Can Be Punished," *Independent*, 10 April 2018, www.independent.co.uk/life-style/gadgets-and-tech/china-social -credit-system-punishments-rewards-explained-a8297486.html.

16. "China: Police 'Big Data' Systems Violate Privacy, Target Dissent," *Human Rights Watch*, 19 November 2017, www.hrw.org/news/2017/11/19/china -police-big-data-systems-violate-privacy-target-dissent.

17. See Mark Bridge, "Scientists Frown at Technology's Ability to Read Facial Expressions," *The Times*, 29 July 2019, www.thetimes.co.uk/article/scientists -frown-at-technology-s-ability-to-read-facial-expressions-6jzsjqxcv.

18. For more detail, see the research paper "Emotional Expressions Reconsidered: Challenges to Inferring Emotion from Human Facial Movements," *Psychological Science in the Public Interest*, vol. 20, no. 1 (2019): 1–68, https://journals.sage pub.com/eprint/SAUES8UM69EN8TSMUGF9/full.

19. Quoted in "How Mass Surveillance Works in Xinjiang, China," *Human Rights Watch*, 2 May 2019, www.hrw.org/video-photos/interactive/2019/05/02 /china-how-mass-surveillance-works-xinjiang.

20. See Robin Barnwell and Gesbeen Mohammad, "Bar Codes and Cameras Track China's 'Lab Rats,'" *The Times*, 14 July 2019, www.thetimes.co.uk

/article/bar-codes-and-cameras-track-china-s-lab-rats-tp9wcc0fbThe Times; see also Maya Wang, "'Eradicating Ideological Viruses': China's Campaign of Repression against Xinjiang's Muslims," *Human Rights Watch*, 9 September 2018, www.hrw.org/report/2018/09/09/eradicating-ideological-viruses/chinas-campaign-repression-against-xinjiangs; Josh Chin and Clément Bürge, "Twelve Days in Xinjiang: How China's Surveillance State Overwhelms Daily Life," *Wall Street Journal*, 19 December 2017, www.wsj.com/articles/twelve-days-in-xinjiang-how-chinas-surveillance-state-overwhelms-daily-life-1513700355.

21. See Chris Buckley and Steven Lee Myers, "China Builds More Secret 'Re-education Camps' to Detain Uighur Muslims Despite Global Outcry over Human Suffering," *Independent*, 10 August 2019, www.independent.co.uk/news/world/asia/xi-jinping-regime-han-chinese-threat-uighur-muslims-persecution-detention-camps-a9051126.html.

22. Quoted in Gerry Shih, "'Police Cloud': Chinese Database Tracks Apps, Car Location and Even Electricity Usage in Muslim Region," *Washington Post*, 2 May 2019, www.washingtonpost.com/world/chinese-database-is-tracking-cellphone-usage-car-location-and-even-electricity-usage-of-xinjiang-residents/2019/05/01/12eb3996-6c8a-11e9-be3a-33217240a539_story.html.

23. Moody, "Big Brother Is Watching Them. And We're Next."

24. Matt Ridley, "Britain Can Show the World the Best of AI," *The Times*, 16 April 2018, www.thetimes.co.uk/article/britain-can-show-the-world-the-best-of-ai-585vsthvn.

25. Mary L. Cummings, "Artificial Intelligence and the Future of Warfare," Chatham House, 26 January 2017, www.chathamhouse.org/publication/artificial-intelligence-and-future-warfare.

26. Michael C. Horowitz, "The Promise and Peril of Military Applications of Artificial Intelligence," *Bulletin of the Atomic Scientists*, 23 April 2018, https://thebulletin.org/landing_article/the-promise-and-peril-of-military-applications-of-artificial-intelligence.

27. See Zachary Fryer-Biggs, "The Pentagon Plans to Spend $2 Billion to Put More Artificial Intelligence into Its Weaponry," *The Verge*, 8 September 2018, www.theverge.com/2018/9/8/17833160/pentagon-darpa-artificial-intelligence-ai-investment.

28. Catherine Clifford, "Bill Gates: A.I. Is Like Nuclear Energy – 'Both Promising and Dangerous,'" *CNBC*, 26 March 2019, www.cnbc.com/2019/03/26/bill-gates-artificial-intelligence-both-promising-and-dangerous.html.

29. Rhys Blakely, "Nobel Peace Prizewinning Doctors Warn Killer Autonomous Robots Must Be Banned," *The Times*, 25 March 2019, www.thetimes.co.uk/article/nobel-peace-prizewinning-doctors-warn-killer-autonomous-robots-must-be-banned-zt63np0t8.

30. For more detail, including the full list, see "Asilomar AI Principles," Future of Life Institute, https://futureoflife.org/ai-principles.

31. "IOE Professor Co-Founds the UK's First Institute for Ethical Artificial Intelligence in Education," UCL Institute of Education, 18 October 2018, www.ucl.ac.uk/ioe/news/2018/oct/ioe-professor-co-founds-uks-first-institute-ethical-artificial-intelligence-education.

32. Yuval Noah Harari, "Yuval Noah Harari on Big Data, Google and the End of Free Will," *Financial Times*, 26 August 2016, www.ft.com/content/50bb4830-6a4c-11e6-ae5b-a7cc5dd5a28c.

CHAPTER SIX

UPGRADING HUMANS

AI began with an ancient
wish to forge the gods.
Pamela McCorduck

From ancient times, the practice of medicine has been devoted to caring for the sick. Yet in relatively recent times, a new direction has emerged – medicine that is devoted to enhancing the healthy (and wealthy, one might add). That is, medicine is no longer simply a matter of healthcare, but of life enhancement geared to make people fitter, more beautiful, more intelligent, more advantaged, less disease-prone, and less likely to die young – in short, more impressive and desirable. As the technology becomes more and more sophisticated, desires are awakened (particularly in the minds of those who might be able to afford it) of major human life upgrades.

WHAT IS DRIVING THE DESIRE TO UPGRADE HUMANS?

Here is Yuval Harari's take on what is driving the attempts to upgrade human beings, from his book *Homo Deus*. In a sweeping assessment of history, somewhat reminiscent of Stephen Pinker's rather optimistic book *The Better Angels of Our Nature*,[1] Harari makes three claims.[2] I wish to make only a few brief comments on them, since the main issue for Harari is not the claims themselves but where he is going with them.

Firstly, he regards war as obsolete in that we are more likely to kill ourselves than be killed in conflict.[3] My immediate reaction is to ask, Who is envisaged here? Is Harari thinking mainly of some countries in the West where there has been a sea change in history as wars are no longer generally regarded as the usual way of resolving international differences? And Europe has certainly seen a lengthy period of peace between the Second World War and the Balkan Wars. Yet at the time of writing, wars are raging in many parts of the world. Not only that, but one can imagine that in war-torn areas, despair is likely to lead to increased suicide rates so that although those who commit suicide are not in the technical sense killed in conflict, they are dead as a consequence of conflict. In addition, Harari's claim is challenged by cyberwar scenarios and the prospect of the increased use of autonomous vehicles and weapons in actual warfare.

Secondly, Harari holds that we are more at risk from weight gain than from starvation.[4] This view that famine is set to disappear seems strangely at odds with the disparity between wealth and poverty underlined by frequent humanitarian and ecological disasters and with the evidence of current daily media reports from Africa. In 2017, the Global Report on Food Crises found that there were 108 million people at risk in 48 countries. One year later, in 2018, an increase was recorded to 124 million people in 51 countries.[5] What is more, the increase was largely

84

attributed to increasing conflict in the affected regions. This can hardly be said to support Harari's first two theses.

Thirdly, and finally, Harari thinks that physical death has been reduced to a mere technical problem that is ripe for solution by medical science.[6] In other words, he thinks that within the not too distant future, although we may die, we shall not have to die. A "cure" for death will be found. As if death were a disease – but is it? I would not be so sure for reasons that will appear later. At any rate, this claim seems very far-fetched.

Harari's claims appear to be highly controversial, maybe even false. Insofar as they contain any truth, they would seem to apply to the richer West much more than to the developing world. They also display a moral optimism that is hard to justify. UK Astronomer Royal Martin Rees fears that without forward-thinking, sensible, and international initiatives to combat global threats such as climate change, nuclear weapons, and biological warfare, future generations may be left with "a depleted and hazardous world."[7] Not exactly the utopian world envisaged by Harari.

In particular, the first claim – or, more precisely, Pinker's version of it – has been subjected to a trenchant critique by John Gray, who says that Pinker's statistics are misleading and his idea of moral progress is wishful thinking and plain wrong. Gray points out that Pinker (and also the ethicist Peter Singer, who supports him) fundamentally misreads the Enlightenment by tracing to it an anti-violence revolution. Gray says that neither Pinker nor Singer make "mention of the powerful illiberal current in Enlightenment thinking, expressed in the Jacobins and the Bolsheviks, which advocated and practised methodical violence as a means of improving society. Like many others today, Pinker's response when confronted with such evidence is to define the dark side of the Enlightenment out of existence . . . Rather than war declining, the difference between peace and war has been fatally blurred."[8]

HARARI'S AGENDA FOR THE TWENTY-FIRST CENTURY

Nevertheless, many people are fascinated by Yuval Harari's notions, and the most important thing about them for our purposes is what he builds on them, especially on the third, which he couches in explicitly atheistic terms, a worldview conviction that forms the background to his and many others' thinking about the future: "Humans don't die . . . because God decreed it, or because mortality is an essential part of some great cosmic plan. Humans always die due to some technical glitch . . . Every technical problem has a technical solution. We don't need to wait for the Second Coming in order to overcome death."[9]

Of course, this is all pure assertion without evidence and raises the question of whether Harari really expects us to be so naïve as to accept it on the basis of his authority. Yet such is the desire to avoid death that many people buy into it; and in light of that, Harari claims that the first major agenda item in the twenty-first century is going to be a serious bid for human immortality that will be given an irresistible momentum by the fear of death ingrained in most humans. That fear is reflected in the decision that some wealthy people have made to have their bodies frozen after death (cryogenics) in the hope that they can be brought back to life when scientists discover how to reboot a frozen brain.

Such ideas are not without precedent. For instance, Nikolai

Fedorov (1829–1903), a Russian Orthodox philosopher, suggested that humans could intervene in their own evolution and so direct it towards physical immortality and even resurrection: "This day will be divine, awesome, but not miraculous, for *resurrection will be a task not of miracle but of knowledge and common labor*."[10] He sounds just like Harari!

Coming into the twentieth century, in 1949 Pierre Teilhard de Chardin, a French Jesuit priest and paleontologist, predicted that rapid technological change would result in a merger of humanity and technology. He believed that this would eventually lead to what he called the "Omega Point," where humanity would merge with the divine – *Homo deus*.

This leads to the second item on Harari's agenda – the intensification of the pursuit of happiness. To fulfil that desire, "it will be necessary to change our biochemistry and re-engineer our bodies and minds[11] ... The second great project of the twenty-first century – to ensure global happiness – will involve re-engineering *Homo sapiens* so that it can enjoy everlasting pleasure."[12] "Having raised humanity above the beastly level of survival struggles, we will now aim to upgrade humans into gods, and turn *Homo sapiens* into *Homo deus*"[13] (but "think more in terms of Greek gods"[14]). Harari thinks this will happen gradually, starting with our voluntary ceding of control of our lives to the smartphone and over time changing ourselves by re-engineering, drugs, etc., until we are no longer recognisably human.[15]

TRANSHUMANISM

This is the transhumanist project whose visionaries' aims are summed up by Mark O'Connell in his book *To Be a*

Machine, which won the Wellcome Book Prize in 2018: "It is their belief that we can and should eradicate aging as a cause of death; that we can and should use technology to augment our bodies and our minds; that we can and should merge with machines, remaking ourselves, finally, in the image of our own higher ideals."[16]

David Pearce, the co-founder of the World Transhumanist Association, similarly argues that transhumanism involves increasing the capacity for pleasure and the radical extension of life in order to enjoy this pleasure indefinitely. Pearce describes this as the "Hedonistic Imperative" and predicts that over the next thousand years, "the biological substrates of suffering will be eradicated completely . . . [and] Post-human states of magical joy will be biologically refined, multiplied and intensified indefinitely."[17]

John Gray, in his very instructive book *Seven Types of Atheism*, says: "Contemporary atheism is a continuation of monotheism by other means. Hence the unending succession of God-surrogates, such as humanity and science, technology and the all-too-human visions of transhumanism."[18] He sees this development as a resurgence of Gnosticism – an ancient heresy that regarded humans as spirits trapped in an evil body from which they need to be liberated – this time around by technology. According to Gray, "Gnosticism is the faith of people who believe themselves to be machines."[19] Gray suggests that transhumanism is essentially techno-monotheism.[20]

This drive to move from the organic to the inorganic was anticipated by C. S. Lewis in his dystopic science fiction novel *That Hideous Strength*, written in 1945. The view is expressed by an academic:

In us organic life has produced Mind. It has done its work. After that we want no more of it. We do not want the world any longer furred over with organic life, like what you call the blue mould – all sprouting and budding and breeding and decaying. We must get rid of it. By little and little, of course. Slowly we learn how. Learn to make our brains live with less and less body: learn to build our bodies directly with chemicals, no longer have to stuff them full of dead brutes and weeds. Learn how to reproduce ourselves without copulation.[21]

As John Gray says, there would appear to be a strong element of Gnosticism in this attitude. In his perceptive review, Giles Fraser writes approvingly of Gray's insistence on "the idea that science or technology can somehow deliver us from the sort of questions that have driven some of us to God – questions about mortality, for instance – is every bit as superstitious as any religious belief. For many, technology and science function in today's society very much the same way as magic once did – they both represent the fantasy that there can be some quick fix to the challenges of being human."[22]

In the same vein, Leon Kass, professor of social thought at the University of Chicago, has given a sober warning regarding this kind of development:

We have paid some high prices for the technological conquest of nature, but none so high as the intellectual and spiritual costs of seeing nature as mere material for our manipulation, exploitation, and transformation. With the powers for biological engineering now gathering, there will be splendid new opportunities for a similar degradation in our view of man ... And clearly, if we come to see ourselves as meat, then meat we shall become.[23]

Kass shows that aspects of the AGI quest are far from being morally innocuous and neutral. It can be seen rather as a quest for mastery and power. The direction in which that power takes us is a matter for profound ethical concern, as C. S. Lewis presciently observed as far back as 1943 in his remarkable book *The Abolition of Man*:

> What we call Man's power over Nature turns out to be a power exercised by some men over other men with Nature as its instrument ... Man's conquest of Nature, if the dreams of some scientific planners are realized, means the rule of a few hundreds of men over billions upon billions of men. There neither is nor can be any simple increase of power on Man's side. Each new power won *by* man is a power *over* man as well. Each advance leaves him weaker as well as stronger. In every victory, besides being the general who triumphs, he is also the prisoner who follows the triumphal car ... Man's final conquest has proved to be the abolition of Man.[24]

C. S. Lewis wrote these words after he had become a Christian, yet atheist John Gray regards them as of prophetic value, even for those who do not share Lewis's theological convictions.[25] Gray also reminds us that the attempt to use science and technology to upgrade humanity is far from new. He cites both the medieval Jewish myth of a human-like being made of dust or mud called the Golem and Mary Shelley's *Frankenstein*, published in 1818. In Gray's view, "the attempt to create an artificial human being risked making a monster."[26]

The history of the twentieth century gives strong support to this view. Two horrific examples come to mind. Firstly, in Germany, where the Nazis imagined they could create an Aryan superhuman by what they called "scientific breeding," a cynical euphemism that involved the killing of people regarded as disposable because they were regarded mentally or physically below standard or "unfit" or "racially impure." Hitler essentially took over the idea of "the survival of the fittest" and applied it to human beings in his quest for the *Übermensch*. That led to the extermination of millions of Jews, Poles, and other "undesirables" in the most depraved violence the world has ever seen.

In the former Soviet Union, attempts were made to use science to create a "New Man." In 1924, Leon Trotsky wrote: "Man will make it his purpose to master his own feelings, to raise his instincts to the heights of consciousness, to make them transparent, to extend the wires of his will into hidden recesses, and thereby to raise himself to a new plane, to create a higher social biologic type, or, if you please, a superman."[27]

What that program of eugenics involved is explained by historian Andrey Zubov as cited by Sergei Gogin:

> "The Soviet man" evolved as a result of a deeply negative selection process, whereby "the best, most honest and most cultured people were either killed or prevented from having a family and raising children by exile or imprisonment, whilst the worst sort of people, namely those who took part in the creation of this new form of man or silently supported the new authorities, could 'be fruitful and multiply.'"[28]

Such horrific examples support John Gray's prediction that the likely outcome of all such attempts to re-engineer humanity will be the extinction of humanity. He comes to a wry conclusion: "For myself, unregenerate humanity is preferable – the flawed and conflicted creatures we are in fact are much more interesting than the transformed creatures we'd like to be. But I'm sure we're not done with trying. For if anything is peculiarly human, it's the refusal to be what we are."[29]

C. S. Lewis developed this theme – which he started in *The Abolition of Man* – in his book *That Hideous Strength* mentioned above. It tells of a sinister scientific institution euphemistically – and cleverly – called N.I.C.E., the National Institute for Coordinated Experiments, which intends to exploit a small university in England as a recruitment centre for highly questionable experiments in vivisection.

Near the beginning of the book, the amoral driving force behind the project, Lord Feverstone, says to one of the central characters, sociologist Mark Studdock: "But it is the main question of the moment: which side one's on – obscurantism or Order . . . If Science is really given a free hand it can now take over the human race and re-condition it: make man a really efficient animal. If it doesn't – well, we're done."[30] Feverstone goes on to say:

> "Man has got to take charge of Man. That means, remember, that some men have got to take charge of the rest . . .
>
> "Quite simple and obvious things, at first – sterilization of the unfit, liquidation of backward races . . . selective breeding. Then real education, including pre-natal education. By real education I mean one that has no 'take

it or leave it' nonsense. A real education makes the patient what it wants infallibly: whatever he or his parents try to do about it. Of course, it'll have to be mainly psychological at first. But we'll get on to biological conditioning in the end and direct manipulation of the brain . . .

"It's the real thing at last. A new type of man: and it's people like you who've got to begin to make him."[31]

Studdock is thus drawn into a gruesome project that turns out to be geared to the conquest of physical death – one of Yuval Harari's agenda items for the twenty-first century.

NOTES

1. Stephen Pinker, *The Better Angels of Our Nature: Why Violence Has Declined* (New York: Penguin, 2012).

2. See Yuval Noah Harari, *Homo Deus: A Brief History of Tomorrow* (New York: HarperCollins, 2017), 1–43.

3. See Harari, *Homo Deus*, 15–16.

4. See Harari, *Homo Deus*, 5–6.

5. See "2018 Global Report on Food Crises," World Food Programme, 21 March 2018, www.wfp.org/publications/global-report-food-crises-2018.

6. See Harari, *Homo Deus*, 22.

7. Martin Rees, *On the Future* (Princeton, NJ: Princeton University Press, 2018), 227.

8. John Gray, "John Gray: Steven Pinker Is Wrong about Violence and War," *The Guardian*, 13 March 2015, www.theguardian.com/books/2015/mar/13/john-gray-steven-pinker-wrong-violence-war-declining.

9. Harari, *Homo Deus*, 22–23.

10. Nikolai Fedorov, "The End of Orphanhood, Limitless Kinship," quoted in G. M. Young, *The Russian Cosmists: The Esoteric Futurism of Nikolai Fedorov and His Followers* (New York: Oxford University Press, 2012), 82, italics original.

11. This calls to mind the more primitive use of the happiness drug soma in Aldous Huxley's 1932 novel *Brave New World*.

12. Harari, *Homo Deus*, 43.

13. Harari, *Homo Deus*, 21.

14. Harari, *Homo Deus*, 47.

15. See Harari, *Homo Deus*, 49.

16. Mark O'Connell, *To Be a Machine: Adventures among Cyborgs, Utopians, Hackers, and the Futurists Solving the Modest Problem of Death* (New York: Anchor, 2017), 2.

17. David Pearce, "The Hedonistic Imperative," www.hedweb.com/hedethic /hedonist.htm.

18. John Gray, *Seven Types of Atheism* (New York: Farrar, Straus and Giroux, 2018), 158.

19. John Gray, *The Soul of the Marionette: A Short Inquiry into Human Freedom* (New York: Farrar, Straus and Giroux, 2015), 10; see O'Connell, *To Be a Machine*, 62; Gray, *Seven Types of Atheism*, 71–93.

20. See Gray, *Seven Types of Atheism*, 66.

21. C. S. Lewis, *That Hideous Strength: A Modern Fairy-Tale for Grown-Ups* (New York: Scribner, 1996), 170.

22. Giles Fraser, "There's More to Atheism Than the Dim-Witted Dawkins Brigade," *UnHerd*, 18 May 2018, https://unherd.com/2018/05 /atheism-dim-witted-dawkins-brigade/.

23. Leon Kass, *Toward a More Natural Science: Biology and Human Affairs* (New York: Free Press, 1985), 76–77.

24. C. S. Lewis, *The Abolition of Man* (1943; repr., San Francisco: HarperSanFrancisco, 2001), 55, 58, 64.

25. See John Gray, "Is It Ever Right to Try to Create a Superior Human Being?" *BBC News*, 6 September 2015, www.bbc.com/news/magazine-34151049.

26. Gray, "Is It Ever Right?"

27. Leon Trotsky, *Literature and Revolution*, trans. R. Strunsky (Chicago: Haymarket, 2005), 207.

28. Sergei Gogin, "Homo Sovieticus: 20 Years After the End of the Soviet Union," *Russian Analytical Digest* 109 (8 March 2012): 13, www.files.ethz.ch/isn/138831 /Russian_Analytical_Digest_109.pdf.

29. Gray, "Is It Ever Right?"

30. Lewis, *That Hideous Strength*, 39.

31. Lewis, *That Hideous Strength*, 40.

CHAPTER SEVEN

ARTIFICIAL GENERAL INTELLIGENCE: THE FUTURE IS DARK?

Artificial Intelligence is the future not only for Russia but for all humankind. It comes with colossal opportunities, but also threats that are difficult to predict. Whoever becomes the leader in this sphere will become the ruler of the world.

Vladimir Putin

Environmental expert James Lovelock, who developed the Gaia hypothesis – the idea that the earth is a self-regulating ecosystem – suggests, in his usual provocative way, that humans may have had their time and should make way for something new. In an interview reported in *The Guardian*, he says: "Because quite soon – before we've reached the end of this century, even – I think that what people call robots will have taken over."[1]

In April 2018 at the TED talks in Vancouver, physicist

and cosmologist Max Tegmark, president of the Future of Life Institute at MIT, made this rather grandiose statement: "In creating AI, we're birthing a new form of life with unlimited potential for good or ill."[2] How much science lies behind this statement is another matter since, to date, all AI and machine learning algorithms are, to quote the neat phrase of Rosalind Picard: "no more alive than Microsoft Word."

A study by Sir Nigel Shadbolt and Roger Hampson entitled *The Digital Ape* carries the subtitle *How to Live (in Peace) with Smart Machines*.[3] They are optimistic that humans will still be in charge, provided we approach the process sensibly. But is this optimism justified? The director of Cambridge University's Centre for the Study of Existential Risk said: "We live in a world that could become fraught with . . . hazards from the misuse of AI and we need to take ownership of the problem – because the risks are real."[4]

The ethical questions are urgent since AI is regarded by experts as a transformative technology in the same league as electricity. The United States and China are determined to dominate the field, and China expects to win by 2030. President Emmanuel Macron wants to make France the AI capital of the world.

It would, however, make more sense to compare AI with nuclear energy than with electricity. Research into nuclear energy led to nuclear power stations, but it also led to a nuclear arms race that almost led the world to the brink of extinction. AI creates problems of similar, or of even greater, magnitude. The brilliant play *Copenhagen* by Michael Frayn explores the question of whether scientists should simply follow the mathematics and physics without regard to the consequences of what

96

they are developing or whether they should have moral qualms about it.[5] The context of the play is the research that led to nuclear fission. Exactly the same issues are raised by AI, except that AI is accessible by many more people than atomic physics and does not need very sophisticated and expensive facilities. You cannot build a nuclear bomb in your bedroom, but you can hack your way around the world and cause substantial damage.

We need to stop and ask: What is the truth behind claims like those of Lovelock and Tegmark? Are they perhaps exaggerated speculation that goes far beyond what scientific research has actually shown? There may well be some validity in the observation that the amount of unjustified speculation claimed for AI is in inverse proportion to the amount of actual hands-on work in AI that the claimant has done. For it would seem that those scientists who actually build AI systems tend to be more cautious in their predictions about the potential of AI than those who do not.

There is also the question of what worldview is driving all of this. What are the assumptions that are being made? Are they in the interests of all of us or simply of an elite few who wish to dominate for their own purposes? The answers given to these questions will depend on the worldview of the participants in AI research, application, and debate who are supplying them. Of particular interest is their view of the nature of ultimate reality. Physicist Sir John Polkinghorne, who once taught me Quantum Mechanics at Cambridge, writes: "If we are to understand the nature of reality, we have only two possible starting points: either the brute fact of the physical world or the brute fact of a divine will and purpose behind that physical world."[6]

ARE BRAINS COMPUTERS?

The main worldview that is behind much writing about the future of humanity is the first of these – atheism. It is expressed by physicist Sean Carroll in his current bestseller *The Big Picture*: "We humans are blobs of organized mud, which through the impersonal workings of nature's patterns have developed the capacity to contemplate and cherish and engage with the intimidating complexity of the world around us . . . The meaning we find in life is not transcendent."[7] Such reductionist physicalism holds that human cognitive abilities have emerged naturally from the biosphere and therefore sees no reason why the same kind of thing can't happen again, once a high enough level of organisation is reached – that is, life emerging from the silicon sphere. Nick Bostrom puts it this way: "We know that blind evolutionary processes can produce human-level general intelligence, since they have already done so at least once. Evolutionary processes with foresight – that is, genetic programs designed and guided by an intelligent human programmer – should be able to achieve a similar outcome with far greater efficiency."[8]

The claim that Bostrom makes in the first sentence here is wide open to challenge, but this is not the place to challenge it.[9] What I am concerned about here is rather the impression that is so easily given by statements like those of Bostrom that the human brain is no more than a computer. It is one thing to say that the brain *functions* in certain ways like a computer. It is an entirely different thing to say that it *is* nothing but a computer. Simulation is not duplication.

We mentioned earlier that the mathematical genius Alan

Turing tried to characterise artificial intelligence in machine terms; an artificial system that could pass as human must be considered as intelligent. For Turing, the test that we now call the Turing Test was limited because of technology. But for the sake of argument, suppose we waive that objection. Suppose we could construct robots that were physically indistinguishable from humans, as in many sci-fi movies, and cognitively at least capable of fooling us. Would that make them actually "intelligent"? I think that it would not. What convinces me of that is the famous Chinese Room experiment – a thought experiment invented by the Berkeley philosopher John Searle. Here is his explanation of it:

The argument proceeds by the following thought experiment. Imagine a native English speaker who knows no Chinese locked in a room full of boxes of Chinese symbols (a data base) together with a book of instructions for manipulating the symbols (the program). Imagine that people outside the room send in other Chinese symbols which, unknown to the person in the room, are questions in Chinese (the input). And imagine that by following the instructions in the program the man in the room is able to pass out Chinese symbols which are correct answers to the questions (the output). The program enables the person in the room to pass the Turing Test for understanding Chinese but he does not understand a word of Chinese.

The point of the argument is this: if the man in the room does not understand Chinese on the basis of implementing the appropriate program for understanding Chinese then neither does any other digital computer solely on that basis because no computer, qua computer, has anything the man does not have.[10]

We must not mistake a computer simulation for the real thing. After all, no one would mistake a computer simulation of the weather for the weather. We should therefore not get confused over simulation of minds.

Distinguished Oxford mathematician Roger Penrose goes even further in arguing that the brain must be more than a computer, since it can do things no computer can even do in theory. Therefore, in his view, no computer can ever simulate the mind. Of course, if *intelligence* is defined – as some people wish – as "the capacity to pass the Turing Test," then I would want to say that humans have something more than the intelligence that AI, no matter how advanced, will never have.

In an article for *Evolution News*, software architect Brendan Dixon wrote: "Computers do not play games like humans play games. Computers do not create like humans create. Computers, at their most fundamental level, do not even solve computational problems like humans solve computational problems." Dixon concluded: "The real problem with AI, then, is . . . the likelihood of our blindly depending on machines, lulled to trust them by bad metaphors. The danger is that computers will fail us, and possibly do so in very bad ways."[11]

Roger Epstein, a former editor of *Psychology Today*, also rejects the assumption that the brain works like a computer. He says:

Forgive me for this introduction to computing, but I need to be clear: computers really do operate on *symbolic representations* of the world. They really *store* and *retrieve*. They really *process*. They really have physical *memories*. They really are guided in everything they do, without exception, by *algorithms*.

Humans, on the other hand, do not – never did, never will. Given this reality, why do so many scientists talk about our mental life as if we were computers?[12]

A neural network can pick out a cat on a YouTube video, but it has no concept of what a cat is. We need once more to remind ourselves that we are not talking about conscious entities. AI expert Margaret Boden, FBA, writes:

Computers don't have goals of their own. The fact that a computer is following any goals at all can always be explained with reference to the goals of some *human* agent. (That's why responsibility for the actions of AI systems lies with their users, manufacturers and/or retailers – not with the systems themselves.) Besides this, an AI program's "goals," "priorities" and "values" don't matter *to the system*. When DeepMind's AlphaGo beat the world champion Lee Sedol in 2016, it felt no satisfaction, still less exultation. And when the then-reigning chess program Stockfish 8 was trounced by AlphaZero a year later (even though AlphaZero had been given no data or advice about how humans play), it wasn't beset by disappointment or humiliation. Garry Kasparov, by contrast, was devastated when he was beaten at chess by IBM's Deep Blue in 1997 ...

Moreover, it makes no sense to imagine that future AI might have needs. They don't *need* sociality or respect in order to work well. A program either works, or it doesn't. For needs are intrinsic to, and their satisfaction is necessary for, autonomously existing systems – that is, living organisms. They can't sensibly be ascribed to artefacts.[13]

The hype in this area is intensified by the fact that terms like "neural networks," "deep learning," and "machine learning" seem to imply the presence of human-like intelligence when these terms essentially refer to statistical methods used to extract probable patterns from huge datasets. The human brain is not a protein nanotech computer! Mathematician Hannah Fry makes a wry and apt comment:

> For the time being, worrying about evil AI is a bit like worrying about overcrowding on Mars. Maybe one day we'll get to the point where computer intelligence surpasses human intelligence, but we're nowhere near it yet. Frankly, we're still quite a long way away from creating hedgehog-level intelligence. So far, no one's even managed to get past worm.[14]

RE-IMAGINING EVOLUTION

Nevertheless, Yuval Harari's optimism knows no bounds. In his bestseller *Sapiens* he writes: "For close to 4 billion years, every single organism on the planet evolved subject to natural selection. Not even one was designed by an intelligent creator . . . The biologists are right about the past, but the proponents of intelligent design might, ironically, be right about the future."[15]

However, could it be that the exact opposite is the case:

that biologists are wrong about the past – in thinking that life came about by mindless, unguided processes?[16] Might not the fact that life depends on information-bearing macromolecules fit much better with the idea that it was designed by a creative intelligence? Is it also possible that the artificial intelligent design proponents might just be wrong about the future – in thinking that the human mind can create artificial life?

In any case, we should note that the first part of Harari's statement ignores the self-evident fact that evolution did not produce life in the first place. The reason is that biological evolution, whatever it does, can only get going when life (*bios*) is already present! You cannot explain the existence of something on the basis of one of its consequences. The fact, now widely acknowledged, is that no one has any real idea how life originated, so, to say the least, Harari is jumping the gun at this point. Nevertheless, in a remarkable display of unjustified hubris, he says: "Now humankind is poised to replace natural selection with intelligent design, and to extend life from the organic realm into the inorganic."[17] He suggests that there will be three main ways of doing this: biological engineering, cyborg engineering,[18] and the engineering of inorganic beings.[19]

In their book *Evolving Ourselves*, Juan Enriquez and Steve Gullans imagine such a world in which evolution no longer depends on natural processes, but rather on human choices, through what they call unnatural selection and nonrandom mutation.[20] Now, it is clear that intelligent design is already making some progress in the direction of upgrading humanity. For instance, Harari told the *Guardian*: "In the 21st century medicine is moving onwards and trying to surpass the norm, to help people live longer, to have stronger memories, to have better control of their emotions. But upgrading like that is not an egalitarian project, it's an elitist project. No matter what norm you reach, there is always another upgrade which is possible."[21]

It is an elitist project since such life-enhancing medical upgrades tend to be expensive. For example, cochlear implants that wire directly into the auditory nerves can transform hearing at the cost of £40,000 each. Brain-computer interfaces (BCIs) are being developed to help disabled people move incapacitated limbs or even their attached robotic prosthetics. They are likely to be very expensive, as is more speculative technology that may eventually be able to establish a direct connection between our brains and the internet.

Surgical enhancement for the wealthy has already become a very big business, and there are now companies that explicitly advertise their expertise in human upgrades. For example, Elon Musk has formed a company, Neuralink, with the goal of fusing the human brain with AI. Scientists have already developed technology that enables paralysed people to type using only their minds. Among non-surgical options, performance-enhancing drugs – like anabolic steroids to build up muscles,[22] stimulants to increase alertness, and human growth hormones to increase strength and endurance – are finding increasingly widespread use particularly in the sports arena, in spite of their potential side-effects and the ethical problems surrounding them.

Looking back over the relatively few developments mentioned here, we see, on the one hand, that a great deal of what has already been done is of considerable positive value, particularly developments like thought-controlled bionic limbs. On the other hand, some research, like that into modifying the human germline, is ethically questionable.

Such progress has the effect of making the advent of AGI more plausible in the eyes of many people. This development, if ever it occurs, would have huge implications, so that it is important to think about it, even if the contours are unclear. One good reason for this is the fact that some aspects of what AGI might do – like the universal surveillance developments mentioned in chapter 3 – are already spreading throughout the world today. Surveillance at the levels intended brings with it immense power; not surprisingly, there is a great deal of literature that addresses the question of eventual world domination in the hands of those who develop AGI, or even in the hands of an AGI system itself. However, we should not let futuristic scenarios blind us to the fact that AI has already gone far enough to make major aspects of world domination realisable within a relatively short time. We do not have to wait for full AGI for that to happen.

SCENARIOS OF WORLD DOMINATION BY AGI

MIT physicist Max Tegmark imagines how world domination might occur in three steps: first make human-level AGI, then use it to create superintelligence, and finally unleash the superintelligence to take over the world.[23]

In the prelude to his book *Life 3.0*, Tegmark imagines a highly secretive AI project run by what he calls the Omega Team, which develops a powerful AI system called Prometheus. This system is initially unleashed to make money by using Amazon's Mechanical Turk (MTurk), which, as Wikipedia explains, is a crowdsourcing internet marketplace enabling individuals and businesses to find people to take tasks that computers are currently unable to do. It is one of the sites of Amazon Web Services. Employers are able to post jobs known as "Human Intelligence Tasks" (HITs). Workers, known as Turkers, can then browse among existing jobs and complete them in exchange for a monetary payment set by the employer.

Tegmark has chosen the name Prometheus for his AGI system rather aptly. Prometheus was the Titan of Greek mythology who, as the Greek poet Hesiod tells us, was thought to have created humans from clay and to have defied the gods and stolen fire that he gave to the humans to drive forward their development. For his transgression, he was punished by Zeus by being chained to a rock, and an eagle was sent to eat his liver each day. It grew again overnight, and the process was repeated. He was often thought of as an exemplar of the possibility of tragic results that could emanate from attempts to improve the human condition. Interestingly, Mary Shelley gave the subtitle *The Modern Prometheus* to her novel *Frankenstein*.

Tegmark's Prometheus surreptitiously replaces the Turker workers with its much faster AI system and, in consequence, begins to harvest vast revenues. The Omegas then train Prometheus to make films, and the revenues increase exponentially. This wealth is then used to take over the world's businesses and media outlets and to influence governments. You can imagine the rest for yourself.

Prometheus eventually ends up in absolute control of the planet: "For the first time ever, our planet was run by a single power, amplified by an intelligence so vast that it could potentially enable life to flourish for billions of years on Earth and throughout the cosmos – but what specifically was their plan?"[24]

The idea is that, in this way, the world would become the perfect totalitarian state – whatever "perfect" means in that context. Not only can Prometheus record all electronic communications – a capacity that many governments have had for years – it can understand all communications and so be fully aware of what people around the world are thinking and doing:

> With the excuse of fighting crime and terrorism and rescuing people suffering medical emergencies, everybody could be required to wear a "security bracelet" that combined the functionality of an Apple watch with continuous uploading of position, health status and conversations overheard. Unauthorized attempts to remove or disable it would cause it to inject a lethal toxin into the forearm.[25]

Now it is clear that Tegmark intends this as an imaginative introductory scenario. It is imaginative in more ways than one. For instance, Prometheus, being a machine, does not *understand* all communication, nor is it *aware* of what people around the world are thinking and doing for the simple reason that it has no mind with which to understand or be aware.

Wisely, Tegmark does not say that this is what he thinks the future will definitively be but rather asks his readers if they think such a future is possible, and if so, would they want it that way. In his view, the future is still ours to write. However, there are three disturbing things about Prometheus that immediately come to mind. Firstly, at least one major part of a very similar scheme is already being implemented – the use of AI-based surveillance systems for widespread social control in China that we described in chapter 3. Secondly, something very similar to

107

Prometheus features in many sci-fi dystopias. One need only to think of such popular movie and television franchises as *The Matrix*, *Blade Runner*, or *Doctor Who*. Thirdly, and most importantly as we shall later see, this kind of scenario was adumbrated centuries ago in the biblical literature.

Tegmark also investigates a wide variety of AGI scenarios that have been suggested by different leading figures in the AGI scene. Some assume that humans will be able to control the superintelligence and possibly use it to eliminate opposition. Another scenario takes the opposite view and imagines that Prometheus breaks out and takes control of humanity and possibly eliminates them.

The question then is: How can we ensure that such a superintelligence will safeguard human interests and not threaten human existence? Putting this another way, we might ask: What worldview will a superintelligence or an AGI have? This is an important question, since that worldview will have to be embedded by the human constructors and software programmers. What might that worldview be and on what values will it be based?

To discuss this comprehensively is beyond our scope here, and the reader is recommended to consult AI researcher David Bell's book, *Superintelligence and World-views*.[26] But long before we get to superintelligence or AGI, if ever we do, it is worth noting the all too human irony of seeming to want as much choice as possible yet abdicating our choice and delegating it to machines that are usually programmed by others and therefore embody their decisions and not ours.

Max Tegmark describes twelve possible scenarios for humanity's future that represent summaries of inputs from many different thinkers.[27] Some of them are optimistic, and others are pessimistic. In some of them, the AGI seems to possess the characteristics of a benevolent god; in others, those of the devil – with all shades in between. Notice that half of these scenarios tend towards the utopian, and half towards the dystopian, so that between them they cover a very large spectrum. Which of the two tendencies is the more likely will depend, at least in part, on the status we give to moral evil.

Tegmark is prudently careful not to commit himself to what will happen or when it will happen.

Rosalind Picard points out that Tegmark does not exhaust the theoretical possibilities.[28] It may be that superintelligence is never created, not because humanity drives itself extinct, but because we develop technology to help people get smarter and able not only to protect each other but also to avoid a grim *1984* scenario.

However, there is an additional consideration. It is easy to imagine that in whatever direction the future develops, progress towards it will be essentially continuous. But in connection with AGI scenarios, that is hardly likely to be the case, as there may come a time in the future, as C. S. Lewis pointed out in his book *The Abolition of Man*, when one generation has the power to alter the nature of all succeeding generations.[29] We now know that this could be done by germline genetic engineering.

If and when that happens, the inevitably few controllers in that age will define the nature of the "humans" of the future that they will create. But as Lewis chillingly says of those controllers and their products: "Nor are their subjects necessarily unhappy men. They are not men at all: they are artefacts. Man's final conquest has proved to be the abolition of Man."[30]

Such a dystopic scenario can be thought of as human beings trying to play the role of *Homo deus*, where *Deus* is a malevolent god. Philosopher J. Budziszewski at the University of Texas writes:

> Genesis, I think, is the crux of it. To abolish and remake human nature is to play God. The chief objection to playing God is that someone else is God already. If He created human nature, if He intended it, if it is not the result of a blind fortuity that did not have us in mind – then we have no business exchanging it for another. It would be good to remember that Genesis contains not only the story of creation but the story of Babel, of the presumption of men who thought they could build a tower "to heaven."[31]

Budziszewski continues in a manner reminiscent of C. S. Lewis:

> You say you want man to be to himself what God has been to man. But what God has been to man is man's absolute superior, and man cannot be his own superior. A thing can be equal to itself, but it cannot be greater than itself. So [what you really mean is] you want some men to be to other men what God has been to man. You want some men to be the absolute superiors of *others*. I assume that you want to be in the former group and not in the latter . . . You say you want to change the human design. But in that case there must be two groups: Those who caused the change, and those who result from it. And the former hold all the cards.[32]

There is no avoiding the topic of God when we think of the future. Two of Tegmark's AGI scenarios even have "God" in their title. Tegmark observes that many people like the "Protector God" scenario because of its similarity to the major monotheistic religions.[33] Let's turn to the biblical source of those religions to see what it has to contribute – and in particular, to the book of Genesis.

NOTES

1. Quoted in Decca Aitkenhead, "James Lovelock: 'Before the End of This Century, Robots Will Have Taken Over,'" *The Guardian*, 30 September 2016, www.theguardian.com/environment/2016/sep/30/james-lovelock-interview-by-end-of-century-robots-will-have-taken-over.

2. Quoted in Matt Ridley, "Britain Can Show the World the Best of AI," *The Times*, 16 April 2018, www.thetimes.co.uk/article/britain-can-show-the-world-the-best-of-ai-585vsthvn.

3. Nigel Shadbolt and Roger Hampson, *The Digital Ape: How to Live (in Peace) with Smart Machines* (Oxford: Oxford University Press, 2019).

4. Quoted in Jane Wakefield, "AI Ripe for Exploitation, Experts Warn," *BBC News*, 21 February 2018, www.bbc.com/news/technology-43127533.

5. Michael Frayn, *Copenhagen* (New York: Bloomsbury, 2017).

6. John Polkinghorne, *Serious Talk: Science and Religion in Dialogue* (Harrisburg, PA: Trinity, 1995), 3.

7. Sean Carroll, *The Big Picture: On the Origins of Life, Meaning, and the Universe Itself* (London: Oneworld, 2016), 3, 5.

8. Nick Bostrom, *Superintelligence* (Oxford: Oxford University Press, 2014), 23.

9. See my book *God's Undertaker* (Oxford: Lion, 2007).

10. "Chinese Room Argument," in *The MIT Encyclopedia of the Cognitive Sciences*, ed. Robert A. Wilson and Frank C. Keil (Cambridge, MA: MIT Press, 1999), 115.

11. Brendan Dixon, "No, Your Brain Isn't a Three-Pound Meat Computer," *Evolution News*, 20 May 2016, https://evolutionnews.org/2016/05/no_your_brain_i.

12. Roger Epstein, "The Empty Brain," *Aeon*, 18 May 2016, https://aeon.co/essays/your-brain-does-not-process-information-and-it-is-not-a-computer, italics original.

13. Margaret Boden, "Robot Says: Whatever," *Aeon*, 13 August 2018, https://aeon.co/essays/the-robots-wont-take-over-because-they-couldnt-care-less.

14. Hannah Fry, *Hello World: Being Human in the Age of Algorithms* (New York: Norton, 2018), 12–13.

15. Yuval Noah Harari, *Sapiens: A Brief History of Humankind* (New York: HarperCollins, 2015), 397, 399.

16. See my book, *God's Undertaker*, 207–10.

17. Yuval Noah Harari, *Homo Deus* (New York: HarperCollins, 2017), 73.

18. Cyborg is a cybernetic organism, usually imagined in terms of a fusion of human and machine – for instance, bionic hands, some versions of which can now be operated by thought alone.

19. See Harari, *Sapiens*, 399–409.

20. Juan Enriquez and Steve Gullans, *Evolving Ourselves: Redesigning the Future of Humanity – One Gene at a Time* (New York: Current, 2015).

21. Ian Sample, "Body Upgrades May Be Nearing Reality, but Only for the Rich," *The Guardian*, 5 September 2014, www.theguardian.com/science/2014/sep/05/body-upgrades-only-for-rich.

22. Used by more than a million Americans according to a 2015 report (see "Performance Enhancing Drugs Market to Witness a Significant Growth in Terms of Value During Forecast Period 2018–2023," *Medgadget*, 10 August 2018, www.medgadget.com/2018/08/performance-enhancing-drugs-market-to-witness-a-significant-growth-in-terms-of-value-during-forecast-period-2018-2023.html.

23. See Max Tegmark, *Life 3.0: Being Human in the Age of Artificial Intelligence* (New York: Knopf, 2017), 134–60.

24. Tegmark, *Life 3.0*, 21.

25. Tegmark, *Life 3.0*, 136.

26. David Bell, *Superintelligence and World-views: Putting the Spotlight on Some Important Issues* (Tolworth: Grosvenor House, 2016).

27. See "Summary of 12 AI Aftermath Scenarios," Future of Life Institute, https://futureoflife.org/ai-aftermath-scenarios; "The Future of AI – What Do You Think?" Future of Life Institute, https://futureoflife.org/superintelligence-survey. For another set of scenarios, set in 2065 – ten years after Ray Kurzweil's purported "singularity" – see the article by Stephan Talty in the *Smithsonian Magazine*: Stephan Talty, "What Will Our Society Look Like When Artificial Intelligence Is Everywhere?" *Smithsonian* (April 2018), www.smithsonianmag.com/innovation/artificial-intelligence-future-scenarios-180968403.

28. Private communication. Used with permission.

29. C. S. Lewis, *The Abolition of Man* (1947; repr., San Francisco: HarperSanFrancisco, 2001), 56.

30. Lewis, *Abolition of Man*, 64.

31. J. Budziszewski, *What We Can't Not Know* (Dallas: Spence, 2003), 56.

32. Budziszewski, *What We Can't Not Know*, 56, 135.

33. Tegmark, *Life 3.0*, 228.

CHAPTER EIGHT

THE GENESIS FILES: WHAT IS A HUMAN BEING?

Before we think of stepping onto an escalator that leads to the technological abolition of human beings that C. S. Lewis predicted, it might be wise to revisit the biblical account of their value and significance. I shall do this from an unashamedly theistic, indeed, Christian, perspective.

My reasons for so doing are threefold. Firstly, much of the literature on this subject is written from an equally unashamed atheistic perspective, and I think that the public deserve to hear that there actually is another point of view and to be exposed to it so that they can make up their own minds. For not all thought-leaders in the field of AI are atheists. For instance, Donald Knuth and Rosalind Picard are Christians, to name but two. Nor should we forget that Charles Babbage, the "father of computing," was also a Christian believer. In his famous *Ninth Bridgewater Treatise*, he wrote: "The object of these pages . . . is to show that the power and knowledge of the great Creator of matter and of mind are unlimited."[1]

Secondly, there is evidence that aspects of the biblical worldview lie at the heart of the professed liberal morality that often claims to have shrugged off that worldview in favour of atheism.[2]

Thirdly, I am convinced that science and the Christian worldview make excellent rational companions, whereas science and the atheistic worldview do not. For instance, science proceeds on the basis of the assumption that the universe is, at least to a certain extent, accessible to the human mind. No science can be done without the scientist believing this, so it is important to ask for grounds for this belief. Atheism gives us none, since it posits a mindless, unguided origin of the universe's life and consciousness.

Charles Darwin saw the problem. He wrote: "With me the horrid doubt always arises whether the convictions of man's mind, which has been developed from the mind of the lower animals, are of any value or at all trustworthy."[3] Similarly, physicist John Polkinghorne says that the reduction of mental events to physics and chemistry destroys meaning: "Thought is replaced by electrochemical neural events. Two such events cannot confront each other in rational discourse. They are neither right nor wrong. They simply happen . . . The world of rational discourse dissolves into the absurd chatter of firing synapses. Quite frankly that cannot be right and none of us believes it to be so."[4]

Polkinghorne is a Christian, but some well-known atheists also acknowledge the difficulty here. John Gray writes: "Modern humanism is the faith that through science humankind can know the truth – and so be free. But if Darwin's theory of natural selection is true this is impossible. The human mind serves evolutionary success, not truth."[5] Another leading atheist philosopher, Thomas Nagel, thinks in the same way. In his book *Mind and Cosmos*, with the provocative subtitle *Why the Materialist Neo-Darwinian Conception of Nature Is Almost Certainly False*, he says: "If the mental is not itself merely physical, it cannot be fully explained by physical science . . . Evolutionary naturalism implies that we should not take any of our convictions seriously, including the scientific world picture on which evolutionary naturalism depends."[6] That is, naturalism, and therefore atheism, undermines the foundations of the very rationality that is needed to construct or understand or believe in any kind of argument whatsoever, let alone a scientific one. In short, it leads to the abolition of reason – a kind of "abolition of man," since reason is an essential part of what it means to be human.

Not surprisingly, I reject atheism because I believe Christianity to be true. But that is not my only reason. I also reject it because I am a mathematician interested in science and rational thought. How could I espouse a worldview that arguably abolishes the very rationality I need to do mathematics? By contrast, the biblical worldview that traces the origin of human rationality to the fact that we are created in the image of a rational God makes real sense as an explanation of why we can do science. Science and God mix very well. It is science and atheism that do not mix.

THE BIBLICAL STORY

The book of Genesis begins the biblical metanarrative that makes most sense to me of God, the universe, and human life. The very first words in Genesis played a key role in the rise of modern science in the time of Galileo, Kepler, and Newton: "In the beginning, God created the heavens and the earth." This tells us that God is primary, the universe derivative. Matter is not the only reality; it is not even the prime reality. The prime reality is God, who is Spirit. This is aptly captured by Keith Ward: "There is at least one mind that is prior to all matter, that is not in time and therefore is not capable of being brought into being by anything. It is the one truly self-existent reality, and the cause of all physical things."[7]

The opening words of Genesis are echoed in another majestic statement with which John's Gospel begins: "In the beginning was the Word, and the Word was with God, and the Word was God. He was in the beginning with God. All things were made through him." This statement will be familiar to Christians, but it may not be familiar to everyone, and, in any case, many Christians may not have grasped its profound implications.

We are familiar with words as a vehicle of self-expression and intelligible communication. The Stoic philosophers among the ancient Greeks who predated the writer John used the term *Word* (*logos* in Greek) to express the rational principle that they regarded as being behind the natural order. John elevates the term even higher to denote God himself as the rational Creator who is responsible for the existence of the universe and all that it contains.

This is a profound assertion about existence. "In the beginning was the Word" – that is, the Word already was. The Word exists eternally. The Word did not come to be. Contrast that with Ray Kurzweil's answer to the question: "Does God exist?" "Not yet," he said, implying, I imagine, that one day humans might create him.[8]

John goes on to say: "All things were made through him." The universe, however, is not eternal. It came to be by means of the creative Word. Indeed, says John, there is nothing that came to be that did not come to be through the Word. The universe did not produce intelligence; it was the intelligence of God the Word that produced the universe.

These statements about the Word correspond to the account in the first chapter of Genesis, where creation is described in six stages or days, each of which begins with the phrase: "And God said" – so that creation occurs in a series of speech acts by an intelligent God. There is an irony here in that those who are seeking to create a superintelligence do not realise that there is good evidence that a superintelligence, *the* superintelligence, already exists: God the Creator and Sustainer of the heavens and the earth.

This universe bears the signature of its superintelligent divine origins in its law-like behaviour, in its rational intelligibility, in the information-rich macromolecules in our DNA, and in the informational structure of intricate physiological mechanisms responsible for, for example, the migration of birds and fish, and in our human capacities for thought and language, feelings and relationships.

Information is now one of the fundamental concepts of science, although it is not physical. The information on this page is carried on the physical medium of paper and ink. But the information itself is not physical, a fact that would appear to create insuperable difficulty for a strictly materialistic understanding of the universe. Not only that, but the immateriality of information presents a categorical barrier to the construction of a material machine (computer) that can consciously understand in any meaningful sense.

Max Tegmark seems to avoid this issue. He obscures the problem by asserting that information is "substrate-independent"[9] – meaning that the same message can be carried on different material substrates; for instance, a menu can be written on paper or slate or can appear on a screen. But that being so, information cannot itself be material, since material is substrate dependent, as it is its own substrate. It is, therefore, surely fair to argue that the informational aspects of the universe, life, and consciousness ultimately point to, and are consistent with, the existence of a non-material source for these things – the Mind of God.[10]

Here are some of the main implications of the account of creation found in Genesis 1.[11]

1. Creation did not occur all at once but involved a sequence of creation steps or days.
2. The sequence has a start and an end – so the past is not likely to be completely explicable in terms of the present. Creation, in the sense of inauguration, is not the same as providence/upholding/causing to exist.
3. Each step in the creation narrative begins with God speaking: "And God said." The universe is not a closed system but an open system built up systematically by a sequence of inputs of the Word at intervals. However long it took, it was clearly the antithesis of a mindless, unguided process.
4. On two days God spoke more than once:

    Day 3 (Genesis 1:9–13): "And God said, 'Let the waters under the heavens be gathered together into one place, and let the dry land appear.' And it was so. God called the dry land Earth, and the waters that were gathered together he called Seas. And God saw that it was good.

"And God said, 'Let the earth sprout vegetation, plants yielding seed, and fruit trees bearing fruit in which is their seed, each according to its kind, on the earth.' And it was so. The earth brought forth vegetation, plants yielding seed according to their own kinds, and trees bearing fruit in which is their seed, each according to its kind. And God saw that it was good. And there was evening and there was morning, the third day."

This suggests that you do not, in spite of what naturalism asserts, get from the inorganic to organic without an external input of information and energy from the Creator: "And God said . . ." Compare with this the goal of AGI to get from inorganic silicon to inorganic silicon-based life by *human* intelligent design.

Day 6 (Genesis 1:24–27, 31): "And God said, 'Let the earth bring forth living creatures according to their kinds – livestock and creeping things and beasts of the earth according to their kinds.' And it was so. And God made the beasts of the earth according to their kinds and the livestock according to their kinds, and everything that creeps on the ground according to its kind. And God saw that it was good.

"Then God said, 'Let us make man in our image, after our likeness. And let them have dominion over the fish of the sea and over the birds of the heavens and over the livestock and over all the earth and over every creeping thing that creeps on the earth.'

"So God created man in his own image,
in the image of God he created him;
male and female he created them . . .

"And God saw everything that he had made, and behold, it was very good. And there was evening and there was morning, the sixth day."

According to this text, then, you do not, in spite of what naturalism asserts, get from animals to humans without an external input of information and energy from God: "And God said . . ." AGI intends to get from human life and intelligence to machine life and intelligence by human technology.

5. The Genesis sequence implies a teleology, a purpose (contrast that with the naturalistic view that denies purpose in biology – and often elsewhere). According to Genesis, humans are made in the image of God. The heavens declare God's glory, but they were not made in his image. You cannot define the human person without referring to the intelligent mind of God. That is, there is no purely "bottom-up," physicalist, reductionist explanation of what a person is, contrary to what Yuval Harari and others imagine.

6. "And God spoke to them." That humans are made in the image of God is seen in the fact that God spoke to them, directing them to reproduce and to be stewards over the created world using the capacities he had given them. In AGI, scientists will "speak" in the sense that they will code information into their artefacts, and so any directing of them will depend on the desires and views of those scientists. This speech, however, will not be bi-directional conscious communication.

It is impossible to exaggerate the importance of the Genesis narrative with its answer to the first major question mentioned in this book: Where do we come from? Far from emerging by unguided natural processes from materials in the early earth, as the Miller-Urey experiment (original or extrapolated) purported to establish (see chapter 2), we come from a superintelligent, superhuman, and eternal God who created us intentionally in his image from materials to be found in the earth.

It is through this lens that we now look at the biblical view of what is involved in human life in the sense of what it is that makes life meaningful, or what it means to be a human person. This I understand to be the subject matter of the second major part of Genesis, which runs from verse 4 of chapter 2 to the end of chapter 4.

This section unpacks the meaning of the image of God that humans bear, and a lot of work needs to be done to think through its implications for artificial intelligence and life, the things that we (might) make in our image. The text mentions a number of aspects of human life and activity:

- made of the dust of the ground (2:7)
- a living organism (2:7)
- possessing an aesthetic sense (2:8–9)
- endowed with curiosity (2:10–14)
- given work to do (2:15, 5)
- a moral being (2:16–17, 9)
- given the potential of relationship (2:18–25)
- tasked with naming the animals (2:19–20)
- capable of developing industry and the arts (4:21–22)

A detailed discussion of every part of this list would require much more space than we can devote to it here.[12] We shall therefore select what is relevant to our main objective.

HUMAN LIFE HAS A MATERIAL BASE

The LORD God formed the man of dust from the ground and breathed into his nostrils the breath of life, and the man became a living creature.
Genesis 2:7

Genesis readily admits that human beings have a material base. God uses pre-existing material to create them. That is, human beings are the result of the mind of God working on pre-existing matter that God originally created. Artificial life, if it ever is made, will be the result of the minds of humans working on pre-existing matter.

This is the ground zero stage, and yet even getting there is faced by apparently unsurmountable difficulty, as the work of chemist James Tour cited earlier shows: "The proposals offered thus far to explain life's origin make no scientific sense. Beyond our planet, all the others that have been probed are lifeless, a result in accord with our chemical expectations. The laws of physics and chemistry's Periodic Table are universal, suggesting that life based upon amino acids, nucleotides, saccharides and lipids is an anomaly. Life should not exist anywhere in our universe. Life should not even exist on the surface of the earth."[13]

Tour is talking about life in its simplest form here. Human life is vastly more complex still, and according to Genesis, it does not come about by self-organisation of the already shaped material base, nor from some electrical or chemical shock, nor from some vague "emergence." We are told that the source of life is the breath of God, a divine intervention, apparently distinct from material creation.

This raises the question: Will humans ever be able, analogously, to breathe the breath of life into any material artefact that they have constructed? In this connection, think of the body of someone who died one second ago. All the material that goes to make up a human being is still there. But the person is no longer alive. Could it be restored in some way? Now, of course, the person may have died from a heart malfunction. Suppose we had a healthy heart available. Would it be enough, say, to quickly replace the heart and then give the body an electric shock? Or suppose we could one day build a human body, chemically, molecule by molecule, so that it lay before us on a table. Could we now get it to live biologically? If not, why not? What exactly is physical life? We simply do not know in any deep sense.

HUMAN BEINGS POSSESS AN AESTHETIC SENSE

And the LORD God planted a garden in Eden, in the east, and there he put the man whom he had formed. And out of the ground the LORD God made to spring up every tree that is pleasant to the sight and good for food. The tree of life was in the midst of the garden, and the tree of the knowledge of good and evil.

Genesis 2:8–9

Here, Genesis draws our attention to the fact that human beings have an aesthetic sense. That presupposes consciousness whose nature is considerably more impenetrable than even physical life, which is difficult enough. Although much research has been done on the neural correlates of consciousness – the way in which parts of the brain "light up" when we are doing a particularly conscious activity – no one knows what consciousness really is. AI has made considerable progress in image "recognition," but this tends to be sophisticated pattern-matching and does not give rise in any sense to the kind of awareness that would imply conscious mental recognition.

The construction of an aesthetically aware robot would be a vast step beyond image recognition and faces huge obstacles, not the least of which is that no one has any idea what conscious awareness is, although there are many grandiose but meaningless statements made about it, like that of Francis Crick: "You, your joys and your sorrows, your memories and your ambitions, your sense of personal identity and free will, are in fact no more than the behavior of a vast assembly of nerve cells and their associated molecules."[14] The logical incoherence of this is obvious – if it were so, how would we even begin to know it?

Getting some kind of understanding of the relationship of the conscious mind to the body is acknowledged by all to be very difficult. The Hebrew word *nephesh* for "breath" used in Genesis is variously translated as "soul," "person," or "self." In the New Testament, Jesus' statement in Matthew 10:28 ("Do not fear those who kill the body but cannot kill the soul. Rather fear him who can destroy both soul and body in hell") shows that the soul is not understood in this text to be the living body, as it cannot be killed by humans. But what is it, more precisely?

Distinguished Christian philosophers Alvin Plantinga, Richard Swinburne, and J. P. Moreland argue that we shall make no real progress in understanding until we are prepared to revive a thoroughgoing substance dualism – that is, to recognise that there is a non-physical aspect to human beings, as Plato argued centuries ago in developing the idea of an immortal soul. Even philosopher David Chalmers, who specialises in this area, though he is strongly inclined to materialism, nevertheless argues: "Reductive explanation of consciousness is impossible and I even argue for a kind of dualism."[15]

The case for dualism is strengthened when we take on board the biblical teaching that matter is not primary but derivative. Spirit is primary. Matter does not generate spirit. It is God, who is Spirit, who generates matter. It is clearly one thing to try to build AI systems that seek to mimic aspects of what the human mind can do; it is an entirely different thing to try to recreate what it feels like to be a human. Consciousness bars the way.

HUMANS ARE CURIOUS

A river flowed out of Eden to water the garden, and there it divided and became four rivers. The name of the first is the Pishon. It is the one that flowed around the whole land of Havilah, where there is gold. And the gold of that land is good; bdellium and onyx stone are there.
Genesis 2:10–12

The Genesis text informs us here that there were four rivers that watered the garden environment. These rivers lead to regions where there is mineral wealth – there is gold, and the gold is good. This prompts us to think about human curiosity, following a river to where it leads, the spirit of exploration, and, more generally, research and intellectual activity of all kinds. Humans are insatiably curious, and satisfying that curiosity is a very important part of life – practically, life itself – for many people, among them many of my colleagues at the University of Oxford. Yet once more we need to face the fact that human curiosity is inextricably linked with human consciousness, and so the way seems barred to making an AI system that reflects this.

UNCOUPLING INTELLIGENCE FROM CONSCIOUSNESS

One of Yuval Harari's contentions is that many people researching into AI do not concern themselves with consciousness for the simple reason that their AI systems are allowing them to create *intelligence (simulated) that is not conscious* – and that is sufficient for their purposes.

It is easy to get some idea of what this means. Suppose I take a taxi journey from the train station to a meeting in Oxford. The taxi driver is conscious – otherwise the journey is rapidly going to run into serious trouble. But if I undertake the journey in an autonomous vehicle, the taxi driver is superfluous. All I need to achieve my goal is an AI system that "knows" the route and can guide the car along it, but there is no need for a conscious driver at any stage. Or suppose I need heart surgery. The last surgeon I experienced was a conscious human being; the next, should I need it, may well be a non-conscious robotic AI system.

Genesis tells us that when God created humans in his image, he *linked intelligence and consciousness together in one being*, for he is himself like that – a conscious intelligent being. However, God, who is Spirit, links consciousness and intelligence together in a non-material being. The fact that God is Spirit shows that neither consciousness nor intelligence necessarily depend on a material substrate – another reason to think that humans will never be able to make a conscious material machine.

HUMANS WERE ASSIGNED WORK

Genesis 2:15 informs us that God gave work, in a garden, as part of the human raison d'être before sin entered into the world. That is why people who try but do not succeed in finding work often feel deprived and unwanted. Yet, work, though very important, is not all of life as it was essentially thought to be in the Communist concept of a "worker state." However, what is happening now is that, as suggested above, by decoupling intelligence from consciousness, AI would seem to be pushing us in the opposite direction to a situation where work becomes a smaller and smaller part of human activity. Even if Ray Kurzweil is overly optimistic in saying that most human tasks will be taken over by robots by 2030, we need to think about what even a partial AI/robot takeover would look like in light of the biblical view that work is part of our God-given significance as human beings.

Yuval Harari writes: "In the twenty-first century we might witness the creation of a massive new unworking class: people devoid of any economic, political or even artistic value, who contribute nothing to the prosperity, power and glory of society. This 'useless class' will not be merely unemployed – it will be unemployable."[16] Digital assistants, robots, and the like can be regarded as slaves, and the world already experienced a slave economy where the very few were served by the many. That very few did little work, and when society collapsed, having forgotten how to work, they had no idea how to rebuild. Some suggest it was for that reason that the Roman Empire eventually collapsed.

The concept of a "useless class" is chilling and dehumanising. The New Testament advice for believers is: "If anyone is not willing to work, let him not eat" (2 Thessalonians 3:10). It does not, however, say, if anyone does not work, let him not eat. It is almost as if Paul envisaged the possibility of unemployment. If certain AGI pundits are right, the prospect of future techno-unemployment is worse than grim.

In chapter 5, we gave some idea of the projected time-scale of job erosion in the survey by the University of Oxford's Future of Humanity Institute. It is obvious that there is an

128

urgent need to create many new jobs, and if they are not to disappear too rapidly, they will have to be jobs that humans can do better than algorithms. This will mean that many, if not most, people will have to keep learning throughout life, a prospect that many will find either daunting or simply impossible.

The techno-optimists hope that even if such people cannot be employed, there will be enough financial surplus from the new technology that they will be fed, housed, and supported throughout life. But who will be paying for the new technological services – certainly not people who have no work? Where will the financial surplus come from? Such techno-optimism seems extremely naive! The extreme techno-pessimist view is, as Nick Bostrom warns, that humans will not in fact reach the final stage of unemployability, as an ascendant AI may well simply exterminate them.[17]

Yet according to Scripture, work is an important ingredient in human flourishing. How can those of us who are convinced of that fact communicate and maintain it in the face of a technological invasion of the workplace? Is our stark choice really between learning to work with robots or being replaced by them?[18] Once AI masters the art of horticulture, will there be a job for Adam?

The problem is huge, and it starts not with retraining those that have already been employed, but with the basic education of children. The World Economic Forum reports:

The jobs of the future will require students to have strong cognitive skills in mathematics and literacy, as well as soft skills such as problem-solving and creative thinking, to enable them to adapt to a quickly changing environment.

However, *millions of children are not gaining these skillsets*, either because they never started school, they have dropped out of school, or their school does not offer a quality education.[19]

It would appear that 617 million children and adolescents fall below an acceptable standard in reading and mathematics.[20] The tragedy here is that this represents an immense waste of talent and leads to severely reduced potential to escape long-term poverty.

It is a sobering thought that AI may leave millions of children far behind, totally unable to compete with the more privileged.

HUMANS HAVE THE FACULTY OF LANGUAGE

God instructed man to name the animals in Genesis 2:19–20. The thought that an AI system might be able to name objects does not sound completely far-fetched since, at the basic level, a name is to a large extent an arbitrary sound attached to the object and then written down. Human capacities, however, go way beyond naming things. Theologian Keith Ward wrote: "There are here three distinctive capacities of the human person, unique among all organisms on Earth, so far as we can tell – the capacity to be sensitive to and appreciative of information received, to be creative in responding to it, and to learn and develop such capacities in relation to other persons in specific historical contexts. Human persons receive information, interpret it, and transmit it in a fully semantic way."[21] This would seem to be in a completely different category from the information-processing ability of computers or the image recognition of AI.

Yet AI systems are already beginning to invade the world of the artist, musician, and writer. At the time of writing (2018), one of the first AI artistic compositions is about to be auctioned at Christie's. David Cope, former music professor at the University of California in Santa Cruz, who writes about AI and music, has developed impressive computer programs to create classical music in the style of any given composer. Audience response has shown that Cope's music is indistinguishable from Bach, for example.

Cope has developed an even more sophisticated machine learning system called "Annie" that not only writes music but also various kinds of poetry. This is slightly misleading since what such a system produces is generated by Cope plus AI, not by AI alone. As Paul Ford, who attempted to write an article using machine learning, has said: "At least for now computers need people as much as we need them."[22] The reason is clear: all of these things are being done by unconscious machines that are, in turn, being guided by conscious humans.

GOD CREATED THE MAN/WOMAN RELATIONSHIP

The Genesis 2 account raises the question of a suitable companion for man. Animals have been human companions from time immemorial, and with advances in medicine resulting in ageing populations, the need for companionship is at an all-time high. That need is being increasingly supplied by lifelike companion robots, and it is spawning a huge industry, particularly in countries like Japan. At the other end of the age scale, robotic ducks have been developed to help children with cancer. Also, healthcare robots that combine AI with voice technology are being developed that will, for instance, remind people to take their medicines at the right time.

However, the biblical account indicates that like-for-like companionship cannot be supplied by a subhuman animal, since there is a category difference between humans and animals – as indicated by the information gap on Day 6 of the creation narrative.

According to the Genesis account, woman, the biblical counterpart of man, is built from man by God. What implications does this have for the way we understand the nature of human-to-human relationships as distinct from interactions with companion robots, robotic pets, robotic house helps, and even life-size robotic dolls? Will they, for instance, even enhanced by AI, one day be capable of responding to the complex blend of emotional, social, cultural, and physical needs of people in a way that satisfies the human need for understanding and compassion?

Margaret Boden points out that other human beings, of course, don't always provide these things either. Yet she goes on to say:

> In a nutshell, over-reliance on computer "carers," none of which can really care, would be a betrayal of the user's human dignity . . . In the early days of AI, the computer scientist Joseph Weizenbaum made himself very unpopular with his MIT colleagues by saying as much. "To substitute a computer system for a human function that involves interpersonal respect, understanding, and love," he insisted in 1976, is "simply obscene."[23]

Boden also issues a warning: "The users and designers of AI systems – and of a future society in which AI is rampant – should remember the fundamental difference between human and artificial intelligence: one cares, the other does not." However, in this context we should balance these comments by referring to Rosalind Picard's positive work in affective computing, mentioned elsewhere, that is very much an expression of AI care – simulated care, but nonetheless care as far as the patient is concerned.

The humans were told to be "fruitful and multiply" (Genesis 1:28) to give life to succeeding generations by the natural process of the sexual transmission of life. Of course, at that stage, there was no question of one generation interfering with the genetic programming of subsequent generations. That would come much later, though thinking about it, as our generation must, will involve the next ingredient in what it means to be human.

NOTES

1. Charles Babbage, *The Ninth Bridgewater Treatise*, 2nd ed. (London: Murray, 1838), ix.

2. See Larry Siedentop, *Inventing the Individual: The Origins of Western Liberalism* (Cambridge, MA: Harvard University Press, 2014).

3. "Letter to William Graham, July 3, 1881," University of Cambridge Darwin Correspondence Project, https://goo.gl/Jfyu9Q.

4. John Polkinghorne, *One World: The Interaction of Science and Theology* (London: SPCK, 1986), 92–93.

5. John Gray, *Straw Dogs: Thoughts on Humans and Other Animals* (London: Granta, 2002), 26.

6. Thomas Nagel, *Mind and Cosmos: Why the Materialist Neo-Darwinian Conception of Nature Is Almost Certainly False* (Oxford: Oxford University Press, 2012), 14, 28.

7. Keith Ward, *Why There Almost Certainly Is a God: Doubting Dawkins* (Oxford: Lion, 2008), 19–20.

8. This was a comment at the end of a documentary entitled *Transcendent Man: The Life and Ideas of Ray Kurzweil* (Los Angeles: Ptolemaic Productions, 2009).

9. Max Tegmark, *Life 3.0* (New York: Knopf, 2017), chapter 2.

10. See my *God's Undertaker* (London: Lion, 2007) or *God and Stephen Hawking: Whose Design Is It Anyway?* (London: Lion, 2011).

11. I go into this in much more detail in my *Seven Days That Divide the World: The Beginning according to Genesis and Science* (Grand Rapids: Zondervan, 2011).

12. But see my *Seven Days That Divide the World.*

13. James Tour, "Open Letter to My Colleagues," *Inference: International Review of Science* 3, no. 2 (August 2017), https://inference-review.com/article/an-open -letter-to-my-colleagues; see also James Tour, "Animadversions of a Synthetic Chemist," *Inference: International Review of Science* 2, no. 2 (May 2016), https://inference -review.com/article/animadversions-of-a-synthetic-chemist.

14. Francis Crick, *The Astonishing Hypothesis: The Scientific Search for the Soul* (New York: Scribner, 1994), 3.

15. David J. Chalmers, *The Conscious Mind: In Search of a Fundamental Theory* (Oxford: Oxford University Press, 1996), xiv.

16. Yuval Noah Harari, *Homo Deus* (New York: HarperCollins, 2017), 330.

17. See Ross Andersen, "We're Underestimating the Risk of Human Extinction," *The Atlantic*, 6 March 2012, www.theatlantic.com/technology/archive/2012/03 /were-underestimating-the-risk-of-human-extinction/253821.

18. See Bill Snyder, "Our Misplaced Fear of Job-Stealing Robots," Stanford Graduate School of Business, 7 March 2019, www.gsb.stanford.edu/insights /misplaced-fear-job-stealing-robots.

19. Silvia Montoya, "There Is a Global Learning Crisis Affecting the Lives of Millions in Developing Countries," World Economic Forum, 27 August 2018, www .weforum.org/agenda/2018/08/global-learning-crisis-millions-without-basic-skills -unesco (emphasis added).

20. See "The Sustainable Development Goals Report 2019: Sustainable Development Goal 4," United Nations, https://sustainabledevelopment.un.org/sdg4.

21. Keith Ward, "God as the Ultimate Informational Principle," in *Information and the Nature of Reality*, ed. Paul Davies and Niels Henrik Gregersen (Cambridge: Cambridge University Press, 2014), 375.

22. Paul Ford, "I Tried to Get an AI to Write This Story," *Bloomberg Businessweek,* 17 May 2018, www.bloomberg.com/news/features/2018-05-17/i-tried -to-get-an-ai-to-write-this-story-paul-ford.

23. Margaret Boden, "Robot Says: Whatever," *Aeon*, 13 August 2018, https:// aeon.co/essays/the-robots-wont-take-over-because-they-couldnt-care-less.

CHAPTER NINE

THE ORIGIN OF THE HUMAN MORAL SENSE

The biblical account of the Garden of Eden is one of the most profound stories in all of literature. It relates how the Creator placed the first humans in a garden paradise that was full of promise and interest. They were free to enjoy the garden and explore it and the regions around it to their hearts' content. It was a place of joy and happiness where they could experience the living friendship and companionship of the Creator himself. Not only that, but as we saw above, they were given the task of naming the animals and so begin the wonderful process of understanding the world around them and capturing that understanding in language and so preserving it.

However, there was an added dimension to the human environment that is absolutely essential for our understanding of the world and ourselves – the moral dimension. It is presented to us in the simplest and clearest of terms, but we would be making a serious mistake if we thought it was simplistic. The humans were free – indeed, encouraged – to eat of all the trees in the garden with one important exception. Here is the relevant passage – Genesis 2:15–17:

> The LORD God took the man and put him in the garden of Eden to work it and keep it. And the LORD God commanded the man, saying, "You may surely eat of every tree of the garden, but of the tree of the knowledge of good and evil you shall not eat, for in the day that you eat of it you shall surely die."

The forbidden tree was not the "tree of knowledge," as many people erroneously think. Rather, it was the "tree of the knowledge of good and evil," which is a very different thing. God was not opposed to knowledge. On the contrary, he wanted his creatures to gain knowledge. The garden was full of potential for learning, exploration, the experience of tending and developing a garden with its many varieties of plants, and giving names to what they discovered. God's desire for them to learn is clear from the fact that he placed them in an environment that was conducive to doing so.

Furthermore, far from diminishing human status, by forbidding one thing, God conferred a unique dignity on humans – that of moral capacity. In order for morality to make sense, humans must have a certain degree of freedom – they were free to eat all that was in the garden. But that is not enough. There must also be a moral boundary that in this case consisted in the forbidding of a single fruit. They were, of course, *able* to eat it; otherwise God's prohibition would have been meaningless. God told them, however, that in the day they did eat it they would surely die.

In spite of that, they did eat it for reasons given to us in the biblical narrative:

> Now the serpent was more crafty than any other beast of the field that the LORD God had made.
>
> He said to the woman, "Did God actually say, 'You shall not eat of any tree in the garden'?" And the woman said to the serpent, "We may eat of the fruit of the trees in the garden, but God said, 'You shall not eat of the fruit of the tree that is in the midst of the garden, neither shall you touch it, lest you die.'" But the serpent said to the woman, "You will not surely die. For God knows that when you eat of it your eyes will be opened, and you will be like God, knowing good and evil." So when the woman saw that the tree was good for food, and that it was a delight to the eyes, and that the tree was to be desired to make one wise, she took of its fruit and ate, and she also gave some to her husband who was with her, and he ate. Then the eyes of both were opened, and they knew that they were naked. And they sewed fig leaves together and made themselves loincloths.
>
> *Genesis 3:1–7*

The Genesis account goes on to relate how the serpent-enemy misrepresented God, suggesting that God wished to limit human freedom by not letting the humans become like God. Now I am well aware that the biblical suggestion here that there exists not only an alien but a malevolent non-human intelligence in the universe frequently attracts ridicule. Yet I find that when astronomers suggest that the galaxy is teeming

137

with all kinds of alien life, many people accept it without batting an eyelid. It would therefore appear that the problem is that people cannot imagine that such an ancient document as the Bible could know anything about these things – and they are probably right, if naturalism is true. But that is precisely the point at issue here: "In the beginning, God created the heavens and the earth" is the first action in the grand biblical metanarrative, which constitutes a head-on challenge to that very naturalism.

Furthermore, as we shall later see, many AGI proponents believe that there will be other kinds of intelligences in the future to which human beings might be subject. If humans will eventually be capable of creating intelligences superior to themselves, and extraterrestrial life already exists as so many think, there is certainly no *a priori* reason apart from prejudice for rejecting the biblical introduction of an intelligent alien. C. S. Lewis puts it this way:

> It is impossible at this point not to remember a certain sacred story which, though never included in the creeds, has been widely believed in the Church and seems to be implied in several Dominical, Pauline, and Johannine utterances – I mean the story that man was not the first creature to rebel against the Creator, but that some older and mightier being long since became apostate and is now the emperor of darkness and (significantly) the Lord of this world . . .
>
> It seems to me, therefore, a reasonable supposition, that some mighty created power had already been at work for ill on the material universe, or the solar system, or, at least,

138

the planet Earth, before ever man came on the scene: and that when man fell, someone had, indeed tempted him . . . If there is such a power, as I myself believe, it may well have corrupted the animal creation before man appeared.[1]

We should at least observe that by introducing an evil alien being that deceived the humans, the Bible is therefore not entirely blaming humanity for what subsequently happened. We are told that this creature "was more crafty than any other beast of the field that the LORD God had made." It turns out to be very different from the other creatures: it is clever and it can speak. It engages Eve in conversation about the significance of eating from the prohibited tree of the knowledge of good and evil. It first questions the prohibition: "Did God actually say, 'You shall not eat of any tree in the garden'?" Eve answers, rather inexactly, by saying that God has forbidden even touching the tree, let alone eating it. The serpent responds with outright denial: "You will not surely die." To this it adds, "God knows that when you eat of it your eyes will be opened, and you will be like God, knowing good and evil."

The serpent thus manages, by a devious manipulation of half-truth and a subtle appeal to her rational interest in food, her aesthetic sense, and her desire for insight and fulfilment – all of them wonderful God-given capacities – to drive a wedge between her and her Creator. The snake's power of persuasion is such that Eve takes the forbidden fruit and offers it to Adam, and they both eat. In that searing moment, they discover that the enlightenment received is far from what they thought they desired. Instead of finding life, they begin to experience death, as God had said they would. They do not at once die in the physical sense. That effect of their action will inevitably ensue in due course.

Human life, as we learn from Genesis 2, has many aspects; its lowest level is physical life, to which we must add those other things that make life life – aesthetic environment, work, human relationships, and a relationship with God. Human death, then, will involve the unweaving of all of this. It will first mean the death of fellowship with God, and the first result of this death is a pathetic attempt to hide from God in the garden. The deadly rupture of fellowship with God will then lead inexorably to all the other levels of death – aesthetic death, death of human relationships, and so on, until we reach the lowest level – physical death that turns our bodies back to molecules of dust.

The progenitors of humanity discovered all too late that the knowledge of good and evil that is gained by rejecting God and doing evil is not the kind of knowledge that you want to have. Instead of happiness, they were plunged into a fractured world full of sadness and despair.

This momentous event, often called the Fall, happened when human beings begin to think of themselves as more than an image of God and desire to be a god: "you will be *like* God." In a word, *Homo deus*. We might do well to be suspicious of the *Homo deus* concept – after all, it was first suggested by a diabolical snake! John Gray says that Yuval Noah Harari himself is one of the few people who realise that transhumanism is an attempt at human self-deification.[2] It is to Genesis that we must look to see where the quest for *Homo deus* begins – with the entry of evil into the world. We should not therefore be too surprised when evil crops up in so many depictions of the future.

Human morality, then, was originally defined in terms of obedience or disobedience to the word of God. It only has significance insofar as the humans could understand what God said and had the capacity to choose either to obey or disobey. This, if true, as I believe it to be, is of crucial importance for the ethical evaluation of AI in the contemporary world. Genesis is here claiming that ethics is not relativistic, nor did it evolve horizontally through social evolutionary processes, as many naturalists claim, though society clearly plays a role at a certain level, but it was transcendent in its origin. Part of the image of God is seen in the fact that humans are moral beings.

Moral convictions are, therefore, to a certain extent hard-wired. It is an observable fact that if you look at cultures of whatever kind around the world, you will find common moral elements like respect for truth, family, property, and tribe – and, indeed, other people – as well as reprehension of murder, lying, stealing, and cheating.

However, when it comes to the ultimate value of a human being and what the ground rules are, for example, for modifying one genetically and technologically, our approach will vary, sometimes greatly, according to whether we believe that human life has the transcendent value of having been made in the image of God, or whether we think it is just sophisticated mud and agree with Richard Dawkins when he says that we live in a world in which there is no justice, "no purpose, no evil and no good," a world in which "DNA just is and we dance to its music."[3] At this level, ethics turn out to be worldview-dependent.

However, it is worth pointing out that it is not only theists who recognise the biblical source of many of the ethical principles and values that we expect to be embodied in civilised society. Indeed, leading German atheist intellectual Jürgen Habermas has given clear warning of the dangers of a shift in our moral base from a Judeo-Christian moral base to the postmodern:

> Universalistic egalitarianism, from which sprang the ideals of freedom and a collective life in solidarity, the autonomous conduct of life and emancipation, the individual morality of conscience, human rights and democracy, is the direct legacy of the Judaic ethic of justice and the Christian ethic of love. This legacy, substantially unchanged, has been the object of continual critical appropriation and reinterpretation. To this day, there is no alternative to it. And in light of the current challenges of a post-national constellation, we continue to draw on the substance of this heritage. Everything else is just idle postmodern talk.[4]

If there is "no alternative to it," then at the very least we should not be afraid to bring that seminal biblical legacy to bear on, for instance, the human rights issues that are thrown up by the kind of AI surveillance society towards which some societies appear to be moving very rapidly.

The disobedience that infected the human race from the beginning was a prideful revolt of the human spirit against the God who created it. When they took the forbidden fruit, they experienced shame, unease, and alienation from God. They were not simply conscious beings; they now had a conscience. The man and woman who had enjoyed the joy and friendship of God now felt that God had become their enemy, and they fled to hide from him.

We humans have been fleeing likewise ever since – a flight that bears within it all the seeds of dystopia. There has lurked in the human heart the suspicion that God, if he exists at all, is innately hostile to us. He does not wish our happiness, well-being, or even protracted existence. Human history shows that we have used our autonomy to get out of control. That is exactly what drives the fears around AI. What if our creations get out of control? Will a superintelligent *Homo deus* do to the rest of us what we have done to God? Philosopher and political theorist Hannah Arendt saw the transhumanism as "a rebellion against human existence as it has been given, a free gift from nowhere (secularly speaking), which he wishes to exchange, as it were, for something he has made himself."[5]

Some people are afraid when they try to imagine the kind of creatures into which we might one day make ourselves. Paula Boddington writes:

> For if we see the Genesis account of the Fall of man as foreshadowing of fears about robots, then Genesis gets the problem exactly right, for exactly the right reasons – it's a worry about autonomy itself: what might robots do if we can't control them fully? Will they adhere to the same value system as us? Will they decide to disobey us? What will our relationship with our creations be? . . . We can thank the Hebrew account of Genesis for pre-warning us thousands and thousands of years ago.[6]

Nick Bostrom says: "We cannot blithely assume that a superintelligence will necessarily share any of the final values stereotypically associated with wisdom and intellectual development in humans – scientific curiosity, benevolent concern for others, ... renunciation of material acquisitiveness, a taste for refined culture or for the simple pleasures in life, humility and selflessness, and so forth."[7] We cannot assume that 2084 will not be worse than Huxley's *Brave New World* or Orwell's *1984*. It is, after all, easy to make the assumption that AI will improve human beings – but that may not necessarily be the case.

As we have seen, Yuval Harari describes AGI as decoupling intelligence from consciousness. Bostrom's statement indicates that AGI may also be decoupled from conscience. However, it is very likely to do things that have ethical ramifications, and *either* it is controlled by humans who furnish it with their ethical concepts – and who knows what they may be – *or* it takes control itself with completely unforeseeable and potentially horrific, even terminal, consequences for humanity. If the latter is the case, then the maker of the system still has the responsibility for the disasters that it occasions in the same way that the maker of an autopilot is responsible for a crash caused by that autopilot after it has been given control of an aircraft.

That is the crucial thing. If the ethical programmers are informed by relativistic or biased ethics, the same will be reflected in their products. For that reason, it is surely important that those with transcendent ethical convictions should have a seat at the ethics table when discussing the potential problems of AI.

It is, of course, difficult to discuss ethical values in connection with a superintelligence since there are no facts but only a plethora of wildly differing hypothetical scenarios. Some people hope that if our approach to superintelligence is via human brain enhancement, then the resulting superintelligence may well share common human values. However, we should not let the scary scenarios disconnect us from the fact that they are mostly speculation. Nor should we let them make us forget to be thankful for good technological progress.

That gives me the opportunity to say that my commitment to the biblical worldview, far from turning me into a Luddite vis-à-vis technology, makes me deeply thankful to God for developments that bring hope to people in this damaged world who would otherwise have none – giving hearing to the deaf, sight to the blind, limbs to the limbless; eradicating killer diseases; and benefiting from a host of other things that represent magnificent work in the spirit of a Creator who has made humans in his image to be creative themselves.

AI APPLIED TO MORALITY

We have seen that AI, like any new technology only perhaps more so, brings with it a whole new raft of moral considerations that may easily seem unsurmountable.[8] For AI computer systems have no conscience, and so the morality of any decisions they make will reflect the morality of the computer programmers – and that is where the difficulties start. How can we be sure that the programmers will build in a morality that is benevolent and humane? Rosalind Picard, director of the Affective Computing Group at MIT, puts it succinctly: "The greater the freedom of a machine, the more it will need moral standards."[9]

Political scientist and author of *The End of History* Francis Fukuyama regards transhumanism as "the world's most dangerous idea" in that it runs the risk of affecting human rights.[10] His reason is that liberal democracy depends on the fact that all humans share an undefined "Factor X" on which their equal dignity and rights are grounded.[11] The use of enhancing technologies, he fears, could destroy Factor X. Indeed, I would want to say that Factor X has actually been defined: it is being made in the image of God. Fukuyama writes:

> Nobody knows what technological possibilities will emerge for human self-modification. But we can already see the stirrings of Promethean desires in how we prescribe drugs to alter the behavior and personalities of our children. The environmental movement has taught us humility and respect for the integrity of nonhuman nature. We need a similar humility concerning our human nature. If we do not develop it soon, we may unwittingly invite the transhumanists to deface humanity with their genetic bulldozers and psychotropic shopping malls.[12]

We have seen that one of the stated goals of transhumanism is not merely to improve but to change human nature – as implied in the very word itself. For many of us, this raises deep ethical and theological concerns.

However, the moral questions do not first arrive when some of the transhumanists' goal are achieved. Many systems already operating or almost ready to be put into operation raise immediate ethical problems. For example, autonomous vehicles are the obvious case. They have to be programmed to avoid hitting obstacles and causing damage. But on what moral principles will the choices involved be based, especially in the case of moral dilemmas – Should a self-driving car be programmed to avoid a child crossing the road if the consequence is that it unavoidably hits a bus queue of many adults? Is there any possibility of getting any kind of consensus here?

These are real questions, not only for Christians, but for people of every viewpoint. In trying to answer them, we shall inevitably meet the widespread view that morality is subjective and relative and so there is no hope of making progress here. However, if morality, if our ideas of right and wrong, are purely subjective, we should have to abandon any idea of moral progress (or regress), not only in the history of nations, but in the lifetime of each individual. The very concept of moral progress implies an external moral standard by which not only to measure that a present moral state is different from an earlier one but also to pronounce that it is "better" than the earlier one. Without such a standard, how could one say that the moral state of a culture in which cannibalism is regarded as an abhorrent crime is any "better" than a society in which it is an acceptable culinary practice?

Naturalism denies this. For instance, Yuval Harari asserts: "Hammurabi and the American Founding Fathers alike imagined a reality governed by universal and immutable principles of justice, such as equality or hierarchy. Yet the only place where such universal principles exist is in the fertile imagination of Sapiens, and in the myths they invent and tell one another. These principles have no objective validity."[13]

Yet relativists tend to argue that since, according to them, there are no moral absolutes, no objective rights and wrongs, no one ought to try to impose his moral views on other people. But in arguing like that, they refute their own theory. The word

147

ought implies a moral duty. They are saying, in effect, that because there are no universal, objective principles, there is a universal moral principle binding on all objectivists, and everyone else, namely that no one ought to impose his moral views on other people. In so saying, relativism refutes its own basic principle.

Moral subjective relativism is not liveable. When it comes to the practical affairs of daily life, a subjectivist philosopher will vigorously object if his theory is put into action to his disadvantage. If his bank manager entertains the idea that there is no such thing as objective fairness and tries to cheat the philosopher out of £2,000, the philosopher will certainly not tolerate the manager's subjectivist and "culturally determined" sense of values.

The fact is, as pointed out by C. S. Lewis, that our everyday behaviour reveals that we believe in a common standard that is outside ourselves. That is shown by the fact that, from childhood on, we engage in criticizing others and excuse ourselves to them: we expect others to accept our moral judgments. From the perspective of Genesis, this is surely precisely what you would expect if human beings are made in the image of God as moral beings and therefore hard-wired for morality.

Oddly enough, AI may be able to support this viewpoint. Think of one of the very successful AI applications in medicine we have mentioned – the accurate diagnosis of a particular disease from learning from a large database of X-rays. Suppose now that we were to build a huge database of moral decisions made by human beings and apply machine learning to them. Many of those decisions, if not most, would be biased in some way or other, and we would have to build in methods of recognising the bias. However, as Lianna Brinded puts it in an article for *Quartz*:

> This is easier said than done. Human bias in hiring has been well-documented, with studies showing that even with identical CVs, men are more likely to be called in for an interview, and non-white applicants who "whiten" their resumes also get more calls.
>
> But of course, AI is also not immune to biases in hiring either. We know that across industries, women and ethnic minorities are regularly burned by algorithms, from finding a job to getting healthcare. And with the greater adoption of AI and automation, this is only going to get worse.[14]

How then do you teach fairness to a computer or program it to overcome racial or gender bias? It will only be possible if the programmers know what these things are and are capable of presenting them in a form that a machine can process. If things go wrong because the system amplifies the bias rather than removing it, we cannot blame a conscienceless machine. Only a moral being, the human programmer, can and should be blamed.

Clearly, this issue is central, but it would nevertheless be fascinating to apply AI in this way to a gigantic crowdsourced database of moral choices to see what commonalities arose. In other words, apply AI to moral decision-making itself as a help to what morality should be programmed into the various kinds of system under development. Of course, this runs the risk of determining morality in a utilitarian manner by majority vote, which, as history shows, is not always a wise thing to do.

THE QUEST FOR IMMORTALITY

There was a second special tree in the Garden of Eden – the tree of life. One result of humans taking the fruit of the tree of the knowledge of good and evil was that they lost their access to the tree of life. This implies that human beings were not intrinsically immortal as created. For the continuation of physical life, they were dependent on regularly eating a particular food, the fruit of the tree of life. Its withdrawal after the Fall meant inevitable, though not immediate, physical death. One cannot help wondering whether the legendary search for the elixir of life in the ancient world and the current search for silicon-based immortality are ultimately rooted in this ancient story.

That would seem to mean that Yuval Harari's claim that death is now a "merely technical problem" is way off the mark. Could Genesis imply that physical immortality in the sense of potentially unending life on earth will forever be beyond our intellectual grasp, so that we will never, as Ray Kurzweil and Stephen Hawking suggest, be able to download the contents of our brains onto silicon and so make ourselves immortal? We shall have more to say about immortality later.

THE HUMANIST DREAM

Yuval Harari, optimistic though he at times appears to be, nevertheless sees a major threat to attempts to realise the dream of immortality and divine happiness. He says that this dream is really nothing more than the traditional aspirations of liberal humanism, a view he defines as follows:

The Liberal Story says that if we only liberalize and globalize our political and economic systems, we will produce paradise on earth, or at least peace and prosperity for all. According to this story – accepted, in slight variations, by George W. Bush and Barack Obama alike – humankind is inevitably marching toward a global society of free markets and democratic politics.[15]

Harari sees this view as the best option available, yet he nevertheless thinks that it is flawed and that it may even contain the seeds of its own destruction. He spends the last part of his book *Homo Deus* arguing that "attempting to realise this humanist dream will undermine its very foundations, by unleashing new post-humanist technologies . . . If the whole universe is pegged to the human experience, what will happen once the human experience becomes just another designable product, no different in essence from any other item in the supermarket?"[16]

One of the foundations to which he refers is the liberal humanistic belief in human free will that, as we have just seen, is a central pillar of the Genesis story. One of his reasons for thinking this is that, in common with many contemporary atheists, he denies free will, holding that it "exists only in the imaginary stories we humans have invented."[17] He holds that free will is an invention of theologians and that it is quite easy to see that it is false: "Humans make choices – but they are never independent choices. Every choice depends on a lot of biological, social and personal conditions that you cannot determine for yourself. I can choose what to eat, whom to marry and whom to vote for, but these choices are determined

151

in part by my genes, my biochemistry, my gender, my family background, my national culture, etc. – and I didn't choose which genes or family to have."[18] He thinks that "the last nail in freedom's coffin is provided by the theory of evolution,"[19] but he is not radical enough to question evolution's capacity to do so – or even tell us what that assertion might mean.

Harari continues: "Doubting free will is not just a philosophical exercise. It has practical implications. If organisms indeed lack free will, it implies that we can manipulate and even control their desires using drugs, genetic engineering or direct brain stimulation."[20] In other words, denying free will removes the barriers to human experimentation in the interests of AGI. It also washes away any meaningful base for ethics and so removes all moral barriers. However, the fairly obvious fact that there are many influences involved in human choice does not rule out the fact that there is sufficient freedom for morality to make sense where in the absence of that freedom it wouldn't. This shows just how important it is that we recover the biblical teaching on this issue. In my book *Determined to Believe*,[21] I set out the arguments for the existence of free will and its implication for the moral status of human beings.

The second foundation of liberal humanism (and also, incidentally, a biblical teaching[22]) that Harari sees as delusional is the concept that each of us is an individual. The Genesis account makes that clear by the dignity conferred on us as individuals by stating that we are made in the image of God. Yet Harari, like many others, denies this dignity in the name of biology, thus opening the door to the individual losing his or her significance in the vast databases that are the food of AI.

We have said that millions of us are willingly engaged in

uploading ever more detailed information about ourselves onto the web in such measure that Facebook or Google, for instance, may well end up knowing much more about us than we know ourselves. Almost unawares, we are already abdicating our decisions to AI systems that know more than we do about virtually everything about us – our preferences; our habits; our jobs; our contacts; our travels; what we eat, wear, read, see, believe; our health – both physical and emotional – and our finances. We consult the web about most things, and we shall inevitably start to allow the web to make our decisions for us.

The danger is that, as individuals, we will in this way lose all our meaning in the incessant maelstrom of data flow. This will spell the end of what Harari calls the humanist religion that is designed to enable humans to create meaning in a universe that actually has no meaning. Harari has grim words to say: "Eventually we may reach a point when it will be impossible to disconnect from this all-knowing network even for a moment. Disconnection will mean death."[23]

This network will include what is called the "Internet of Things" that connects all the physical sensors in our gadgets, homes, cars, and environment – and connects them to human beings themselves. There are many tragic examples of young people who are so desperate for acceptance on social media that when their so-called "friends" desert them, or when they are victims of cyberbullying, they feel there is nothing left to live for and commit suicide. The statistics make depressing reading: "Teens' use of electronic devices including smartphones for at least five hours daily more than doubled, from 8 percent in 2009 to 19 percent in 2015. These teens were 70 percent more likely to have suicidal thoughts or actions than those who reported one hour of daily use."[24] Yes – disconnection even from one aspect of the "all-knowing network," social media, can mean death.

Harari's final comment in a 2018 article for *The Guardian* entitled "The Myth of Freedom" makes interesting reading since he thinks, on the one hand, that liberal democracy is flawed, yet, on the other hand, he defends it against what he calls "religious and nationalistic fantasies":

> How does liberal democracy function in an era when governments and corporations can hack humans? What's left of the beliefs that "the voter knows best" and "the customer is always right"? How do you live when you realise that you are a hackable animal, that your heart might be a government agent, that your amygdala might be working for Putin, and that the next thought that emerges in your mind might well be the result of some algorithm that knows you better than you know yourself? These are the most interesting questions humanity now faces.[25]

I am surprised that Harari thinks that these questions are not only important but the *most important*. For there is nothing new here. People have been hacking and using their sales and marketing techniques and spin to influence our amygdalas long before AI came along.[26] What about the far more important questions of why we are here; where we are heading; how we can reduce poverty, loneliness, disease, and the increasing depression and despair in our society, and promote growth, learning, giving, and human connection?

Might there be an alternative way forward in which we

could get involved that would give us answers to those questions? On the first page of his book *Homo Deus*, Yuval Harari writes: "I encourage all of us, whatever our beliefs, to question the basic narratives of our world, to connect past developments with present concerns, and not to be afraid of controversial issues."[27]

Following this encouragement, I wish to question his narrative and introduce one that is completely different, far more radical, and far more likely to be true since it is strongly evidence-based and not one of the "changing social constructs" or "nostalgic fantasies of nationalism or religion" Harari points to.[28] What is more, it is full of hope.

NOTES

1. C. S. Lewis, *The Problem of Pain* (1940; repr., New York: Macmillan, 1962), 133–35.

2. John Gray, *Seven Types of Atheism* (New York: Farrar, Straus and Giroux, 2018), 68.

3. Richard Dawkins, *River out of Eden: A Darwinian View of Life* (New York: Basic, 1995), 133.

4. Jürgen Habermas, *Time of Transitions* (New York: Polity, 2006), 150–51.

5. Hannah Arendt, *The Human Condition* (Chicago: University of Chicago Press, 1958), 2–3.

6. Paula Boddington, "Myth and the EU Study on Civil Law Rules in Robotics," *Ethics for Artificial Intelligence*, 12 January 2017, www.cs.ox.ac.uk/efai/2017/01/12 /myth-and-the-eu-study-on-civil-law-rules-in-robotics.

7. Nick Bostrom, *Superintelligence* (Oxford: Oxford University Press, 2014), 115–16. Note that many of these are in our Genesis list!

8. As a general reference in this area, see David Gooding and John Lennox, *Doing What's Right: Whose System of Ethics Is Good Enough?* book 4 in *The Quest for Reality and Significance* (Belfast: Myrtlefield, 2018).

9. Rosalind Picard, *Affective Computing* (Cambridge, MA: MIT Press, 1997), 134.

10. See Michael Cook, "Is Transhumanism Really the World's Most Dangerous Idea?" *Mercatornet*, 20 July 2016, www.mercatornet.com/articles/view

/is-transhumanism-really-the-worlds-most-dangerous-idea/18394; see also Francis Fukuyama, "The World's Most Dangerous Ideas: Transhumanism," *Foreign Policy* 144, no. 1 (September 2004).

11. See Francis Fukuyama, *Our Posthuman Future: Consequences of the Biotechnology Revolution* (New York: Farrar, Straus and Giroux, 2002), 149–51.

12. Francis Fukuyama, "Special Report: Transhumanism," *FP*, 23 October 2009, https://foreignpolicy.com/2009/10/23/transhumanism.

13. Yuval Noah Harari, *Sapiens* (New York: HarperCollins, 2015), 108.

14. Lianna Brinded, "How to Prevent Human Bias from Infecting AI," *Quartz*, 20 March 2018, https://qz.com/1232285/ad-week-europe-2018-risk-and-rewards -of-ai-and-using-machine-learning-to-remove-bias/.

15. Yuval Noah Harari, "Does Trump's Rise Mean Liberalism's End?" *New Yorker*, 7 October 2016, www.newyorker.com/business/currency/does-trumps -rise-mean-liberalisms-end.

16. Yuval Noah Harari, *Homo Deus* (New York: HarperCollins, 2017), 279.

17. Harari, *Homo Deus*, 285.

18. Yuval Noah Harari, "Yuval Noah Harari: The Myth of Freedom," *The Guardian*, 14 September 2018, www.theguardian.com/books/2018/sep/14 /yuval-noah-harari-the-new-threat-to-liberal-democracy.

19. Harari, *Homo Deus*, 285.

20. Harari, *Homo Deus*, 288.

21. John C. Lennox, *Determined to Believe? The Sovereignty of God, Freedom, Faith, and Human Responsibility* (Oxford: Lion, 2017).

22. It is not unreasonable to argue that the biblical worldview presents a true humanism in that by holding that humans are made in the image of God, it gives them a much higher value than does the (atheistic) humanist philosophy that is widely believed today.

23. Harari, *Homo Deus*, 349.

24. Associated Press, "Rise in Teen Suicide Connected to Social Media Popularity: Study," *New York Post*, 14 November 2017, https://nypost.com/2017/11/14 /rise-in-teen-suicide-connected-to-social-media-popularity-study.

25. Harari, "Yuval Noah Harari: The Myth of Freedom."

26. See Robert B. Cialdini, *Influence: The Psychology of Persuasion* (New York: HarperCollins, 1993).

27. Harari, *Homo Deus*, quote in front matter of the book.

28. Patrick Freyne, "Yuval Noah Harari: 'It Takes Just One Fool to Start a War,'" *The Irish Times*, 30 August 2018, www.irishtimes.com/culture/books/yuval -noah-harari-it-takes-just-one-fool-to-start-a-war-1.3610304.

CHAPTER TEN

THE TRUE
HOMO DEUS

The quest for upgrading humans, creating superintelligence and godhood, is very ancient and, in its contemporary form – dressed up in the language of advanced computer technology – very alluring. The project sounds like the culmination of billions of years of development, initially blind and natural and finally directed by the human mind to which those evolutionary processes gave rise.

Yet at its heart, it delivers a flawed narrative that is neither true to the past nor to the nature of reality. Indeed, its narrative is the reverse of what actually is the case. Superintelligence and godhood are not the end products of the trajectory of the history of human ingenuity. If there is a God who created and upholds the universe and who made us in his image, then a superintelligence, God himself, has always existed. He is not an End Product. He is the Producer.

THE BIBLICAL PERSPECTIVE ON SUPERINTELLIGENCE

In light of what many are now prepared to believe about transhumanism and AGI, it is surely not unreasonable to ask that we at least listen to the biblical perspective on superintelligence and compare it with other scenarios on offer. I would be sad if my sceptical, agnostic, or atheist readers switched off at this point. Not that you owe me anything, but I have spent a great deal of time attempting to understand what you write, and I would hope that you in turn might be interested in hearing how my view interacts with yours.

As we have seen, there appears to be as yet little, if any, evidence or even consensus of belief that AGI will ever be reached. In contrast, there is a great deal of evidence and a widespread conviction that Jesus Christ is both man and God (*Homo + Deus*). This is, of course, a staggering claim. If true, it at once implies that we do not have to wait for some kind of merger of human life and technology to reach a different kind of being with hitherto unprecedented powers. Such a *human* superintelligence already exists. This is in fact the central claim of Christianity as encapsulated in a statement in the Gospel of John about the Word: "The Word became flesh and dwelt among us" (John 1:14). It is an unashamedly supernatural claim that the Word, who is God and never came to be, came to be human. The uncertain quest to enable humans to become gods pales into insignificance with this true narrative that flows in the exact opposite direction – the staggering fact that God has already become man.

PHYSICAL DEATH IS NOT SIMPLY A TECHNICAL PROBLEM: THE SIGNIFICANCE OF THE RESURRECTION OF CHRIST

One of the most important pieces of evidence for the truth of the claim that God became human involves calling into question Yuval Harari's assertion that physical death is simply a technical problem that will yield to medical advance within the next hundred years. Not so. Human death is much more than a technical problem. It is inevitable as a result of the initial rebellion of humans against God (the Fall) and the consequent removal by God of the tree of life. That makes it unlikely that Harari, or anyone else, will ever find that tree, however hard they try.

In any case, the Christian message is that physical death has already been vanquished in the sense that Jesus rose from the dead. His resurrection was not a result of advanced medical technology or biological engineering, but of the direct action of God's divine power. The universe is not a closed system of cause and effect. It is an open system, created by a God who can and does get involved in its operation, sometimes in spectacular special ways in order to draw our attention to his existence, power, and, indeed, care.

I can well understand a sceptical reader baulking at the very idea of a resurrection, although I confess to finding it odd that some who so do seem to have no difficulty in believing that death will one day be overcome by technology. Be that as it may, it is important to say at this stage that Christians make the claim that Jesus rose physically from the dead because it is backed up by strong evidence – both objective in terms of history and subjective in terms of experience.

Not surprisingly, that evidence cannot be reduced to sound-bites. It would require several chapters to do it justice, and since I have rehearsed the main lines of evidence for the resurrection of Christ in the last two chapters of my book *Gunning for God*,[1] it would not be appropriate to reproduce them here. It is sufficient to say that one of the foremost contemporary historians and experts on the New Testament, N. T. Wright, concludes that "the historian, of whatever persuasion, has no option but to affirm both the empty tomb and the 'meetings' with Jesus as 'historical events' ... I regard this conclusion as coming in the same sort of category, of historical probability so high as to be virtually certain, as the death of Augustus in AD 14 or the fall of Jerusalem in AD 70."[2]

The Christian message does not, however, stop with the raising of Christ from the dead. Rather, that is where it starts. For the resurrection of Christ has a major implication for us in the present – that we humans can share in his resurrected life. This is a vastly bigger thing than a human upgrade involving AI. It is, in fact, God's answer to the serpent's taunt that launched the whole human *Homo deus* project in the first place: "You will be like God." For as we have already indicated, one major consequence of the temptation and fall of humanity is that, deep in the human psyche, is embedded the idea that God, if there is one, is against us human beings, against our moving up in the scale of being, against upgrades, against knowledge and all that is associated with fulfilling human potential for flourishing. And because God is against us, we need to snatch at godhood when we get the chance.

This is not true; indeed, to be blunt, it is the lie of all lies, and millions of people have fallen for it. For far from being against us, God wishes to share not only his image with us, as he did in creation, but his life, so that we can become not simply his creatures but his sons and daughters. This has all the potential of a real enhancement.

THE TRIUMPH OF HUMANITY PREDICTED

In those far-off days at the time of the initial human rebellion, God promised a way of salvation from the destructive effects of that rebellion and the alienation between humans and God that it brought with it. To the serpent that had tempted the first humans, God said, "I will put enmity between you and the woman, and between your offspring and her offspring; he shall bruise your head, and you shall bruise his heel" (Genesis 3:15).

This is not merely saying that God would eventually triumph; it is saying that humanity would eventually triumph. This is the start of what might well be called "the Seed Project," *seed* being another term for "offspring." God would eventually bring into the world a particular human, Jesus Christ, who would simultaneously be the seed of the woman (truly human) and the Son of God (truly God). He is the true *Homo Deus*, not an amalgam of human biological life and technology (another human creation), not a man who had been deified like a Roman emperor, but something in a different category altogether – Deity embodied in man, the God Man, Jesus Christ. He is the one who shall ultimately triumph.

The divinely guided historical process that brought him into the world was spread over many centuries because of the preparatory lessons that humanity needed to learn. It involved a sequence of individual human beings who are of great interest in their own right in terms of what they learned of God and what they have passed on to us. To name just a few: Adam, Abraham, Isaac, Jacob, Judah, David, Mary – and, finally, Jesus.

As that process ran its course, predictions about this special "seed" became more and more detailed in their focus. At this point, a sceptical reader may be inclined to say: "But surely you don't take that kind of thing seriously?" I do, but not because I have forgotten my scientific education and descended into irrationality. Indeed, if there is a God who has created this universe and has sustained it ever after, it is not at all implausible to think that his relationship to time is not the same as ours, that he has an overarching knowledge perspective on history and that he is able to be causally involved in the unfolding of events.

The other reason for taking biblical prophecy seriously is its uniqueness as a historical phenomenon. There is so much of it whose fulfilment can be pinpointed, and it does not take much statistical insight to realise the extreme prior improbability of so many long-range predictions being fulfilled so accurately especially if you assume a naturalistic worldview like that of Yuval Harari: "Just as people were never created, neither, according to the science of biology, is there a 'Creator' who 'endows' them with anything. There is only a blind evolutionary process, devoid of any purpose, leading to the birth of individuals."[3] Indeed, fulfilled biblical prophecy provides strong evidence against Harari's beliefs and for the truth of Christianity, so we shall give some examples.

After all, any consideration of AGI involves making predictions about the future, and since we are going to look at such predictions regarding our human future and compare them with the biblical material, it is important that we get some idea of the reliability of the Bible on that score. The Christian claim is that the Bible has been making predictions over the course of centuries whose fulfilments can be checked against the unfolding narrative of the Bible and historical events.

Starting with the offspring or seed of the woman, God tells Abraham, "I will bless those who bless you, and whoever curses you I will curse; and all peoples on earth will be blessed through you" (Genesis 12:3 NIV). Its final fulfilment was announced by the apostle Peter in the early days of the Christian church: "You are heirs of the prophets and of the covenant God made with your fathers. He said to Abraham, 'Through your offspring all peoples on earth will be blessed.' When God raised up his servant, he sent him first to you to bless you by turning each of you from your wicked ways" (Acts 3:25–26 NIV).

It took many centuries to get there, and along the way we get hints of what will one day be. The promise to Abraham was certainly not fulfilled in full in Isaac, yet Isaac carried the promise to his son Jacob, and one of Jacob's sons, Joseph, saved the Egyptian empire and surrounding countries from starvation. This was a huge blessing to the nations but still only a part-fulfilment of the promise. Centuries later, God spoke to Israel's king David through Nathan the prophet:

When your days are fulfilled and you lie down with your fathers, I will raise up your offspring after you, who shall come from your body, and I will establish his kingdom. He shall build a house for my name, and I will establish the throne of his kingdom forever. I will be to him a father, and he shall be to me a son. When he commits iniquity, I will discipline him with the rod of men, with the stripes of the sons of men, but my steadfast love will not depart from him, as I took it from Saul, whom I put away from before you. And your house and your kingdom shall be made sure forever before me. Your throne shall be established forever.

2 Samuel 7:12–16

Some of this promise to David was fulfilled in his son Solomon. But the promise of a throne established forever was not. That fulfilment came with the angel's message to Mary: "You will conceive and give birth to a son, and you are to call him Jesus. He will be great and will be called the Son of the Most High. The Lord God will give him the throne of his father David, and he will reign over Jacob's descendants forever; his kingdom will never end" (Luke 1:31–33 NIV).

These texts introduce us to a very common and important feature of biblical prophecy – short- and long-term fulfilment. Solomon was the short-term fulfilment of the promise to King David. His reign, initially glorious, was marred by unwise behaviour for which God had to discipline him. Jesus Christ is the long-term fulfilment.

In the millennium between David and Christ, the idea of the seed morphed into that of the Anointed One, the Messiah. Many prophets kept the expectation of his coming alive by giving more and more detail as the time of Christ's coming into the world drew near.

For instance, Isaiah (ca. 700 BC) predicted that the Messiah would have a forerunner:

A voice of one calling:
"In the wilderness prepare
the way for the LORD;

> make straight in the desert
> a highway for our God.
> Every valley shall be raised up,
> every mountain and hill made low;
> the rough ground shall become level,
> the rugged places a plain."

Isaiah 40:3–4 NIV

And when John the Baptist came seven centuries later and was asked to identify himself to the Jewish authorities, he replied in the words of Isaiah: "I am the voice of one calling in the wilderness, 'Make straight the way for the Lord'" (John 1:23 NIV).

Micah (who lived around the same time as Isaiah) said that the coming ruler would be born in Bethlehem: "But you, Bethlehem Ephrathah, though you are small among the clans of Judah, out of you will come for me one who will be ruler over Israel, whose origins are from of old, from ancient times" (Micah 5:2 NIV; we should note the hint at the promised ruler's divine origin in the last clause). This prophecy specifying the birthplace of Messiah was accepted by the authorities at the time of Jesus' birth, as we see from their reply to a query addressed to them by King Herod:

> When he had called together all the people's chief priests and teachers of the law, he asked them where the Messiah was to be born. "In Bethlehem in Judea," they replied, "for this is what the prophet has written:
>
> > "'But you, Bethlehem, in the land of Judah,
> > are by no means least among the rulers of Judah;

for out of you will come a ruler
 who will shepherd my people Israel.'"
Matthew 2:4–6 NIV

Isaiah also predicted the birth of a uniquely special child who would be called Immanuel – "God with us": "Therefore the Lord himself will give you a sign: The virgin will conceive and give birth to a son, and will call him Immanuel" (Isaiah 7:14 NIV). That prophecy was fulfilled around seven centuries later when an angel said to the virgin Mary, "The Holy Spirit will come on you, and the power of the Most High will overshadow you. So the holy one to be born will be called the Son of God" (Luke 1:35 NIV). The Hebrew word translated "virgin" in Isaiah's prophecy is *almah*, which means a young woman; however, Luke's translation is the Greek word for "virgin." Now Luke was well aware that this word was likely to cause offence to those of his readers who were conservative Jews, and therefore he would not have used it unless he believed it to be a true description of Mary.

The prophet Zechariah (ca. 520 BC) even specified the manner in which the Messiah would later come into Jerusalem as king: "Rejoice greatly, Daughter Zion! Shout, Daughter Jerusalem! See, your king comes to you, righteous and victorious, lowly and riding on a donkey, on a colt, the foal of a donkey" (Zechariah 9:9 NIV). Jesus deliberately fulfilled this prophecy on his last journey to Jerusalem:

Now when they drew near to Jerusalem and came to Bethphage, to the Mount of Olives, then Jesus sent two disciples, saying to them, "Go into the village in front of you, and immediately you will find a donkey tied, and a colt with her. Untie them and bring them to me. If anyone says anything to you, you shall say, 'The Lord needs them,' and he will send them at once." This took place to fulfill what was spoken by the prophet, saying,

> "Say to the daughter of Zion,
> 'Behold, your king is coming to you,
>> humble, and mounted on a donkey,
>> on a colt, the foal of a beast of burden.'"

The disciples went and did as Jesus had directed them. They brought the donkey and the colt and put on them their cloaks, and he sat on them. Most of the crowd spread their cloaks on the road, and others cut branches from the trees and spread them on the road. And the crowds that went before him and that followed him were shouting, "Hosanna to the Son of David! Blessed is he who comes in the name of the Lord! Hosanna in the highest!" And when he entered Jerusalem, the whole city was stirred up, saying, "Who is this?" And the crowds said, "This is the prophet Jesus, from Nazareth of Galilee."

Matthew 21:1–11

One of the most important Messianic predictions is the famous "Suffering Servant" prophecy of Isaiah (Isaiah 53). It tells us that the Messiah, when he came, would be despised and rejected and suffer as a sacrifice for sin:

> But he was pierced for our transgressions;
>> he was crushed for our iniquities;

upon him was the chastisement that brought us peace,
    and with his wounds we are healed.
All we like sheep have gone astray;
    we have turned – every one – to his own way;
and the LORD has laid on him
    the iniquity of us all.

Isaiah 53:5–6

This passage is cited six times in the New Testament: Matthew 8:14–17; John 12:37–41; Luke 22:35–38; Acts 8:26–35; Romans 10:11–21; and 1 Peter 2:19–25. Luke 22 is of particular importance, since there Jesus cites Isaiah 53:12 as speaking of himself. It is hard for us to resist the overwhelming impression that this text from Isaiah constitutes a vivid and accurate depiction of the rejection, suffering, death – and, indeed, resurrection (verse 12) of Jesus.

However, for the first disciples the hard thing was to accept the fact that Jesus would be rejected and murdered. That was because Jewish understanding of the prophecies at the time was that Messiah would come as a powerful king and free them from the oppression of the Roman occupying power. That Messiah should be rejected and suffer was a contradiction in terms for the Jewish people for the obvious reason that a dead Messiah would be useless in a power struggle.

Thus, when Jesus said he was going to be crucified in Jerusalem, the disciples protested. And when they saw it was actually going to happen, they deserted him. That was not a programme of events that they wished to buy into. They were incapable of grasping why Jesus needed to suffer since they expected Messiah to give the nation its political freedom, and partly in consequence of this, they failed to identify Messiah with Isaiah's Suffering Servant.

The fact is that we humans need saving from our sins much more than we need political freedom or upgrading. Programmes of education and technological or medical upgrades will never adequately deal with moral failure because the root of that failure is a fundamental alienation from God. Christ offers to deal with that alienation by offering us salvation based on his death on the cross for our sins and on his resurrection.

But salvation is not conferred automatically. In order to receive it, we must have a radical change of mind. That is, we must personally repent of the mess we have made of our own and other people's lives.[4] We must turn away from sin and, as an act of our will and heart, trust Christ as Saviour and Lord: "To all who did receive him, who believed in his name, he gave the right to become children of God" (John 1:12).

The transhumanist *Homo deus* project could be seen as a parody of this Christian teaching. We are born as creatures of God. We have to *become* children of God by trusting Christ. The *Homo deus* project seeks to upgrade us; God gives us new life. Christ himself describes this life as eternal life, God's life in us, untouchable by death. We are connected to other believers by the fact that we share a common life and express it in live, face-to-face fellowship in communities called churches, insofar as we are able.

Now, technological connectedness through email, Facebook, WhatsApp, etc. has clearly been a great comfort and help to people who are not mobile, are ill, shut-in, or living in remote communities. The sad thing, though, is that for many able-bodied people, the increase in technological connectedness has gone hand in hand with a decrease in them spending actual time talking to each other and doing things together. Thus, loneliness may, for some, be alleviated, at least partially, with technical connection, whereas for others, exactly the opposite is true.

What God offers is a real, indeed a spectacular, upgrade, and it is credible, since by contrast with hoped-for AI upgrades, it does not concentrate merely on technological improvements, but on the moral and spiritual side of human character. Putting it another way, post-human scenarios tend to be utopian almost by definition, and as we well know, utopian thinking has usually led in the past, not to a promised paradise on earth, but to indescribable violence, war, and the deaths of millions. The reason for that is promises of Utopia are inevitably doomed if they are made without any realistic programme for dealing with the sinfulness of human nature and without pointing people to a source of inner power to help them navigate the complexities of life.

By contrast, Christianity does know of such a power, and the brilliant ancient historian Luke tells us about the advent of that power at Pentecost in the opening chapters of his book of Acts.[5]

For forty days after the resurrection, Jesus met with his disciples, presenting them with convincing evidence that he was alive after having been dead. During that time, he taught them about his kingdom, finally commanding them to go to Jerusalem and wait for the Holy Spirit to come from him to empower them to be his witnesses to the ends of the earth.

They were understandably very interested in what Jesus intended to do next. They wished to know if, now that he had conquered death, he was going to use this power to eject the

Roman occupying power and take over the government as King Messiah. His answer was a clear no. He was not going to restore the kingdom to Israel at that time. One day he would – after all it was a key biblical expectation that Messiah would do just that – but not yet. Furthermore, he was not going to tell them when that event would happen. Their immediate prior task was not to speculate about the future but to be his witnesses around the world. He was about to leave and return to heaven, from where he had originally come.

Luke tells us that as Jesus said this, he rose into the heavens and then a cloud received him out of their sight. They stared, incredulous, into the sky, but were immediately informed that one of the purposes of the ascension was to demonstrate to them not only that he would return, but how he would return. They had seen him go into another world visibly and physically; he would one day come back to this world in exactly the same way, physically and visibly.

We pause to contrast this with the hope of AGI that one day we will be able to upload the contents of our minds onto silicon and so "live" forever. Jesus' mind was not uploaded onto silicon; he ascended bodily into heaven. This claim clashes head-on with the dominant earthbound, atheistic naturalism of the Western academy that teaches that this world is all that there is; there is no other world to which one can ascend. But as I have repeatedly argued elsewhere, naturalism is not true and, contrary to widespread opinion, is not supported by science, but rather undermines it.[6] The promises of AGI are firmly rooted in this world, and in that sense they are parochial and small compared with the mind-boggling implications of the resurrection and ascension of Jesus.

NOTES

1. John C. Lennox, *Gunning for God: Why the New Atheists Are Missing the Target* (Oxford: Lion, 2011).

2. N. T. Wright, *The Resurrection of the Son of God* (Minneapolis: Fortress, 2003), 709–10.

3. Yuval Noah Harari, *Sapiens* (New York: HarperCollins, 2015), 109.

4. That is, confess to God that what we have done is wrong and express the desire to change, with his help, our attitudes and behaviour to comply with his standards.

5. See Acts 1:1–11; 2:1–47.

6. See my *Gunning for God* and *Can Science Explain Everything?* (Epsom, Surrey: Good Book, 2019).

CHAPTER ELEVEN

FUTURE SHOCK: THE RETURN OF THE MAN WHO IS GOD

Before his death, Jesus told his disciples that he was going away but would one day come back for them to take them to a place he was going to prepare for them in the presence of his Father (John 14:1–4). They initially did not understand what he was talking about, but with his resurrection and ascension, it all became much clearer.

CHRIST'S TEACHING ABOUT THE FUTURE

With Jesus' death and resurrection, God's great project for the redemption of the world took an immense step forward as the apostle Peter announced in his second major sermon recorded in the book of Acts. Peter and John healed a lame man at the gate of the temple, and this attracted a large crowd. Peter then publicly explained the significance of the miracle, putting it into the context of what had been happening in Jerusalem in the previous days. Peter directly accuses the crowd of killing the "Author of life" (Acts 3:15) and yet appeals to them by giving them a way out of their dire predicament:

> "And now, brothers, I know that you acted in ignorance, as did also your rulers. But what God foretold by the mouth of all the prophets, that his Christ would suffer, he thus fulfilled. Repent therefore, and turn back, that your sins may be blotted out, that times of refreshing may come from the presence of the Lord, and that he may send the Christ appointed for you, Jesus, whom heaven must receive until the time for restoring all the things about which God spoke by the mouth of his holy prophets long ago."
>
> *Acts 3:17–21*

It was a devastating indictment of those who murdered Jesus, but it was also a gracious offer of salvation for those willing to repent and trust him. Peter answers the unspoken question (Where is Jesus, then?) by pointing out that he had gone to heaven and would remain there until the next great step in God's programme happened – the restoration that will be triggered by Jesus' return.

Sadly, the public face of Christianity has become so insipid and watered down that the vibrant central hope of the return of Christ that should be at its heart has been all but lost – or relegated to the lunatic fringe of naive prophecy mongers. The warning of C. S. Lewis is ignored: "Do not attempt to water Christianity down. There must be no pretence that you can have it with the Supernatural left out. So far as I can see Christianity is precisely the one religion from which the miraculous cannot be separated. You must frankly argue for supernaturalism from the very outset."[1]

Inevitably, one of the consequences of the Enlightenment's rejection of the supernatural was that, as David Bosch says: "Little room was left for the 'great eschatological event Christians had long awaited, namely the Second Coming.' Belief in Christ's return on the clouds was superseded by the idea of God's kingdom in the world which would be introduced step by step through successful labors in missionary endeavor abroad and through creating an egalitarian society at home."[2]

Behind this kind of thinking lies the notion of progress that marked the Enlightenment and the great strides that were made in science, technology, and industry that brought so much wealth to Europe. Unbridled optimism in human potential reigned, and a brave new world was just around the corner. But the imagined Marxist Utopia that was to arise out of the workings of the inexorable laws of history turned into a nightmare of human carnage and cost the lives of millions. Not only Marxism of course. Extreme nationalism of different kinds has produced similar results. History has taught the hard lesson: there is no pathway to paradise that bypasses the problem of human sin.

Nevertheless, well-known Harvard psychologist Stephen Pinker thinks that violence is decreasing, specifically as a result of Enlightenment thinking, a view that John Gray, a British professor of the history of European thought, is swift to rebut in his review of Pinker's book, *The Better Angels of Our Nature*.[3] In his review entitled "Stephen Pinker's Delusions of Peace," Gray writes:

Like other latter-day partisans of "Enlightenment values," Pinker prefers to ignore the fact that many Enlightenment thinkers have been doctrinally anti-liberal, while quite a few have favoured the large-scale use of political violence . . .

The idea that a new world can be constructed through the rational application of force is peculiarly modern, animating ideas of revolutionary war and pedagogic terror that feature in an influential tradition of radical Enlightenment thinking.[4]

The word *Utopia* means "no place"[5] and is, ironically, highly appropriate in this context. Every attempt so far to realise Utopia has failed because the visionaries who tried to create such a state did not take into account the fact that human nature is seriously flawed as a result of the entry of sin and alienation into the world at the Fall. They did not see, as we pointed out earlier, that humans need saving much more than they need upgrading. The utopian visionaries had no message of salvation, no connection with a divine power capable of changing what human beings are like. As a result, the twentieth century was the bloodiest in history.

Pinker thinks violence will decline. Gray thinks not, and in this he is in line with biblical teaching. Jesus himself issued warnings about future events that are as much a part of his teaching as is the Sermon on the Mount. He spoke of the risk of deception by imposters and false prophets who, amidst a rising tide of wars, famines, and earthquakes, will lead many astray. All this will build to a climax towards the end:

"Then will appear in heaven the sign of the Son of Man, and then all the tribes of the earth will mourn, and they will see the Son of Man coming on the clouds of heaven with power and great glory. And he will send out his angels with a loud trumpet call, and they will gather his elect from the four winds, from one end of heaven to the other."

Matthew 24:30–31

Jesus said these things 2,000 years ago, and the intervening time has been characterised by "wars and rumors of wars" (Matthew 24:6). But according to Jesus, these things are not evidence of the end – he explicitly says that such things will happen, but the *end is not yet*. The end of history as we know it will not occur until certain specific things happen that will culminate in the cataclysmic return of Christ to rule.

It is vitally important that those of us who are Christians are not embarrassed at the return of Christ, since he himself made it a central plank in his teaching. He not only taught his disciples in private that he would return; he made it a key point at his trial when questioned about his identity:

Again the high priest asked him, "Are you the Christ, the Son of the Blessed?" And Jesus said, "I am, and you will see the Son of Man seated at the right hand of Power, and coming with the clouds of heaven." And the high priest tore his garments and said, "What further witnesses do we need? You have heard his blasphemy. What is your decision?" And they all condemned him as deserving death.

Mark 14:61–64

The high priest regarded Jesus' reply as blasphemous because he and all the court understood that Jesus was citing a famous passage from the book of the prophet Daniel that referred to a divine Son of Man who would come on the clouds of heaven and be given universal authority and power to reign forever:

> "I saw in the night visions,
>
> and behold, with the clouds of heaven
>   there came one like a son of man,
> and he came to the Ancient of Days
>   and was presented before him.
> And to him was given dominion
>   and glory and a kingdom,
> that all peoples, nations, and languages
>   should serve him;
> his dominion is an everlasting dominion,
>   which shall not pass away,
> and his kingdom one
>   that shall not be destroyed."
>
> *Daniel 7:13–14*

The return of Christ is not some peripheral, add-on idea concocted by hotheads in backstreet fringe sects. It is evident from what occurred at Jesus' trial that he was crucified precisely because he claimed to be the august Son of Man who, according to the prophet Daniel, would one day come on the clouds of heaven to take up universal rule.[6] And because his return is an essential part of the hope he held out to the world, not surprisingly, the New Testament has much to say about it.

THE TRUE SOLUTION TO YUVAL HARARI'S "TECHNICAL PROBLEM" OF PHYSICAL DEATH

God will eventually deal with physical death, but not by solving it by technological means, as Yuval Harari suggests. Firstly, by the raising of Jesus from the dead, God has demonstrated that physical death is not insuperable. The New Testament says that God "has destroyed death and has brought life and immortality to light through the gospel" (2 Timothy 1:10 NIV). Death is not going to have the last word. Christ's bodily resurrection is but the beginning of the restoration of the human race and of the whole of creation, which will happen at his return.

Furthermore, by his death and resurrection, Christ frees from the fear of death all those who trust him:

> Since therefore the children [i.e., Jesus' disciples] share in flesh and blood, he himself likewise partook of the same things, that through death he might destroy the one who has the power of death, that is, the devil, and deliver all those who through fear of death were subject to lifelong slavery.
>
> *Hebrews 2:14–15*

We must be careful to understand exactly what this passage is saying. It is not claiming that those who trust Christ will not experience fear or the onset of illness, severe pain, and the physical anguish of the process of dying. Fear of these things is a natural, automatic reflex action of our human make-up, part of the preservative mechanisms built into our bodies, so that nature itself fights against dying.

People are afraid of death for two opposite reasons. Firstly, some fear that there is nothing after death. Therefore, this present life is all there is, and so, rather than lose physical life, some people will compromise loyalty to God, to truth, to faith, to honour, to principle, and even descend to shameful cowardice – anything to save physical life. Fear of death holds them in moral slavery.

Secondly, other people are afraid of death, not because they think that there is nothing after death, but because they are afraid that there will be far too much after death for their liking, namely, a Final Judgment with eternal consequences.

Christ's death and physical resurrection as a real human being combine to deliver believers from both of these fears. Firstly, it frees them from a sense of hopelessness at the death of a loved one by informing them that their loved one, now "absent from the body" *is* "present with the Lord" (2 Corinthians 5:8 KJV), or as the Lord himself expressed it: "with me in Paradise" (Luke 23:43). It is also the secret of the courage of Christian martyrs who are prepared to die rather than deny Christ.

Christ's death also frees those who trust him from the second kind of fear. They have God's assurance that Christ, by his sacrificial death, has paid in full the penalty for their sins.[7] Physical death comes but once, and the Judgment comes *after* death. For believers, Christ's death atones for their sin – that is, it covers every sin of theirs that the Judgment could take cognizance of. In consequence, believers are given the following magnificent assurance: "Just as it is appointed for man to die once, and after that comes judgment, so Christ, having been offered once to bear the sins of many, will appear a second time, not to deal with sin but to save those who are eagerly waiting for him" (Hebrews 9:27–28). And Christ, who himself will be the final Judge (John 5:22), declares: "Truly, truly, I say to you, whoever hears my word and believes him who sent me has eternal life. He does not come into judgment, but has passed from death to life" (John 5:24).

And now comes the solution to one of Harari's key problems of the twenty-first century – conquering physical death. However, death will not be overcome by medical advances. The good news is that Christ's bodily resurrection instils into everyone who believes in him sure and certain hope of their own eventual bodily resurrection. To get this spectacular truth across to us, Christ's own resurrection is referred to by Paul as the firstfruits of a great harvest to come (1 Corinthians 15:20). Just like the early pickings of fruit promise more fruit to come, so the resurrection of Jesus heralds a great harvest that will take place at Christ's Second Coming – a resurrection of all persons of all centuries who are Christ's. Those who have died before that Coming will be resurrected; those who are still alive at that Coming will be changed without dying. All will be given bodies like Christ's glorious resurrection body (1 Corinthians 15:50–57; Philippians 3:20).

This means for believers, as it did for Christ, that there is to be a physical embodiment after death. One interesting aspect of this in view of the attempt to make silicon-based life is the hint in the New Testament that Jesus' resurrected body was not exactly the same as the body that was buried. It had new properties – it could pass through closed doors, for instance, so that, in a way, it appeared to belong to a different dimension.

In 1 Corinthians 15, Paul contrasts the natural body with

181

the resurrected spiritual body. A spiritual body does not mean a body made in some sense of spirit any more than a petrol engine means an engine made of petrol. Jesus told his disciples he was no spirit: "A spirit does not have flesh and bones as you see that I have" (Luke 24:39). If we put this alongside Paul's statement that "flesh and blood" shall not inherit the (future) kingdom of heaven, then we see that he is indicating that there is a physical difference between the human body as it is now and what it one day will be. My continued existence as *me* is guaranteed, but it will not depend on the development of technology to upload the contents of my brain onto silicon.[8]

Some people think that the idea of bodily resurrection is absurd, since when we die, the atoms of our bodies disperse and become part of the surrounding vegetation, and so may well subsequently become part of other animals and even other humans. How then, they argue, can it make sense to talk about a bodily resurrection of the dead? But this objection seems to overlook certain important facts.

To start with, it is true that at death the atoms in our bodies disperse. But, of course, we do not have to wait until death for this to happen. The cells (and therefore the atoms) in our bodies are constantly changing and dispersing. None of the cells now present in my body were present in my body ten years ago (except, perhaps, certain specialised cells in the brain). Yet in spite of this constant change and replacement of atoms and cells, and in spite of ageing, the formal identity of my body remains recognisably the same. Clear evidence of that is given by the fact that a person's fingerprints (which are unique to that person) remain the same throughout their lifetime (apart, of course, from scarring or mutilation). This fact, first demonstrated by Sir Francis Galton in 1888, plays a decisive role in the identification of culprits. Similar things could be said about identification using DNA.

The complex coding, and whatever else is responsible for maintaining the identity of a body through its time on earth, is known by God for every human being who has ever lived. At the future resurrection, God, who, after all, created matter in the first place, will not be hard up for whatever substance in which the unique bodily identity of each person will be expressed. The result will be that each individual believer will have a body like Christ's glorious resurrection body (and therefore with capacities and glories that our present bodies do not have). But each person will be individually identifiable through the unique form of their resurrection body as the same person who was identifiable by their body here on earth:

> Just as we have borne the image of the man of dust, we shall also bear the image of the man of heaven.
>
> I tell you this, brothers: flesh and blood cannot inherit the kingdom of God, nor does the perishable inherit the imperishable. Behold! I tell you a mystery. We shall not all sleep, but we shall all be changed, in a moment, in the twinkling of an eye, at the last trumpet. For the trumpet will sound, and the dead will be raised imperishable, and we shall be changed . . . This mortal body must put on immortality.
>
> *1 Corinthians 15:49–53*

The deduction that each individual believer is taught to make from the certainty of bodily resurrection is that life in this present body in this world is worth living to the full of one's energies, abilities, and circumstances, in spite of all life's pains and sufferings, old age and eventual death: "Therefore ... be steadfast, immovable, always abounding in the work of the Lord, knowing that in the Lord your labor is not in vain" (1 Corinthians 15:58). This means that, though our bodies here on earth, inherited as they are from a fallen race, are subject to decay and death, what each person does in the body is eternally significant.

As a further example, we might consider the apostle Paul when he visited Thessalonica and preached there for three weeks or so – not a particularly long time. Yet as he reminded them in a letter he subsequently wrote, during that brief visit he told the Thessalonians about the coming of Christ in considerable detail. In fact, their conversion to Christianity was described by some as follows:

> For they themselves report concerning us the kind of reception we had among you, and how you turned to God from idols to serve the living and true God, and to wait for his Son from heaven, whom he raised from the dead, Jesus who delivers us from the wrath to come.
>
> *1 Thessalonians 1:9–10*

In fact, at the end of each chapter of his letter, Paul encourages the believers to live their lives in light of the future coming of Christ. This, together with some of the parables of Jesus that emphasise the unexpectedness and suddenness of his coming – "The Son of Man is coming at an hour you do not expect" (Matthew 24:44) and the statement by Christ in Revelation: "Surely I am coming soon" (22:20) – has erroneously led some people to think that Jesus led the early Christians to expect his return almost immediately, and when this did not turn out to be the case, the hope of such a return faded into the background. However, Jesus himself, in Matthew 24, had warned that the time-scale would be long rather than short. The reason for this apparent paradox is not far to seek: emphasising only a long time-scale might lead some, as some of the parables suggest, to think: "my master is staying away a long time" (verse 48 NIV), and that therefore their behaviour didn't matter.

The resolution of the paradox is surely this: we all move towards the return of Christ at two "speeds" – the speed of earth history and the speed with which we approach death. Jesus and his apostles were not cheating when they encourage believers to live as though Christ could return at any time, as this is the only way to live that will allow our expectation of his coming to have the moral and spiritual effect it should have on us. If I die today, the time of Christ's coming measured in years AD is irrelevant to me.

It was, however, inevitable in those early days, when believers began to die and there was no sign of Christ's return, that questions would be asked about them. In response, at the very end of his first letter to the Thessalonians, Paul reassures the living believers:

> But we do not want you to be uninformed, brothers, about those who are asleep, that you may not grieve as others do who have no hope. For since we believe that Jesus died and rose again, even so, through Jesus, God will bring with him

those who have fallen asleep. For this we declare to you by a word from the Lord, that we who are alive, who are left until the coming of the Lord, will not precede those who have fallen asleep. For the Lord himself will descend from heaven with a cry of command, with the voice of an archangel, and with the sound of the trumpet of God. And the dead in Christ will rise first. Then we who are alive, who are left, will be caught up together with them in the clouds to meet the Lord in the air, and so we will always be with the Lord. Therefore encourage one another with these words.

1 Thessalonians 4:13–18

Paul expected Christians who lost loved ones to grieve but not to grieve in the same way as people who had no hope. To cut through their tears, he gives them more detail about what the return of Christ will mean both for their departed loved ones and for themselves. Paul's own understanding of death was to be "absent from the body" and "present with the Lord" (2 Corinthians 5:8 KJV), and his great hope expressed here is that one day all believers will be with the Lord – and some of them will not even experience physical death at all! This is way beyond anything AI could even dream of.

AI may well make many good and helpful advances that will improve the lot of humanity. However, no matter what the promise might be, the central claim of Christianity is that the future is far greater than anything AI or AGI can promise since something infinitely bigger than either of them *has already happened* on our planet: God, who is responsible for the existence of the universe and its laws and the architecture of the human mind, the divine Logos who was in the beginning, has coded himself into humanity – the Word became flesh and dwelt among us. This is not artificial intelligence; this is Real Intelligence – way beyond anything conceivable, let alone constructible, by humans.

And the fact that God did become human is the greatest evidence of the uniqueness of human beings and of God's commitment to embodied humanity. Humans, original version, are demonstrated to be unique precisely because God could and did become one. And those of us who have received him will one day at his return be gloriously "upgraded" to be like him and share in the marvels of the eternal world to come.

This was the plan from the beginning – and it has implications for the new heaven and the new earth. And since this new creation has a physical dimension, what might we be then allowed to create in the way of heavenly technology?

All of this means that Christians (and indeed others) need to think hard about the implications of these fundamental Christian doctrines of the resurrection and return of Christ for AI and the race to create *Homo deus*. For if the Christian teaching is true, the race to conquer death as a technical problem will prove to be ultimately futile, although the technology developed along the way may help ease old age and solve many outstanding medical problems. However, humans were not made to live indefinitely on this planet. Something much bigger is possible that makes Yuval Harari's scheme seem rather insignificant.

BIBLICAL PERSPECTIVES ON THE ADVENT OF A PERSON CLAIMING TO BE *HOMO DEUS*

Let us now see what the Bible has to say about what is to happen on this planet in the future. John Gray picks up a comment by Yuval Harari that *Homo deus* will resemble the Greek gods and concludes: "Humans may well use science to turn themselves into something like gods as they have imagined them to be. But no Supreme Being will appear on the scene. Instead there will be many different gods, each of them a parody of human beings that once existed."[9]

Gray, who otherwise has many valuable things to say, is wrong here. According to the biblical narrative, history is leading up to the appearance of a Supreme Being, one who has already been here and who, when he was here, promised to return. That fact was, as we have seen, a fundamental part of Christian teaching. It also has major implications for the world, as we see from the second letter Paul wrote to the church at Thessalonica. Apparently, false teachers had turned up in that city who were perverting the Christian message by infecting it with erroneous ideas such as asserting that Christ had already returned. Not only that, but the church was bravely holding out against intensified persecution (2 Thessalonians 1:4). On hearing of this development, Paul wrote to them once more.

As we read what he said, we should bear in mind what we mentioned earlier that, according to the book of Acts, Paul spent only three weeks or so in Thessalonica, yet he felt it was important for those converted to Christianity in that short time to know about the future in some considerable detail. Here is what he wrote:

Now concerning the coming of our Lord Jesus Christ and our being gathered together to him, we ask you, brothers, not to be quickly shaken in mind or alarmed, either by a spirit or a spoken word, or a letter seeming to be from us, to the effect that the day of the Lord has come. Let no one deceive you in any way. For that day will not come, unless the rebellion comes first, and the man of lawlessness is revealed, the son of destruction, who opposes and exalts himself against every so-called god or object of worship, so that he takes his seat in the temple of God, proclaiming himself to be God. Do you not remember that when I was still with you I told you these things? And you know what is restraining him now so that he may be revealed in his time. For the mystery of lawlessness is already at work. Only he who now restrains it will do so until he is out of the way. And then the lawless one will be revealed, whom the Lord Jesus will kill with the breath of his mouth and bring to nothing by the appearance of his coming. The coming of the lawless one is by the activity of Satan with all power and false signs and wonders, and with all wicked deception for those who are perishing, because they refused to love the truth and so be saved.

2 Thessalonians 2:1–10

Paul reminds them that on his first visit to them he had carefully explained that Christ would not return until certain things had happened – things that would be so publicly visible, striking, and obvious that you wouldn't need to be told about them. Recall that Jesus himself said this in the Olivet Discourse in Matthew 24, warning us that many would turn up saying that they were the Christ but that we shouldn't listen to them since the true Christ will return under circumstances that will be spectacularly obvious. Nevertheless, it would appear that false teachers had turned up in Thessalonica who were unsettling the believers by contradicting Christ's teaching and suggesting that the Day of Judgment had already come.

Such erroneous teaching made life even more difficult for the Christians who were suffering persecution at the time. Paul was quick to reassure them that although the Judgment Day had not yet come, it one day would, and in such a manner as to put an end to persecuting powers.

The trigger for the events that Paul mentions here are a rebellion and the appearing of a person described as the "man of lawlessness" (2 Thessalonians 2:3), whose main characteristic is opposition to gods in any shape or form, who nevertheless proclaims himself to be God. Again, no one will fail to recognise this development since, as Paul tells us, this tyrannical leader will be energised by Satanic power and enabled to deceive people by lying wonders. The climax will come when the returning Christ bursts onto the scene and destroys him by his appearing. Clearly nothing on this scale had yet happened in Paul's day, and it has clearly not happened subsequently. Its intensity and global dimensions ensure that when it does happen, the whole world will be all too aware of it.

This scenario is just as far as it could be from the view that Christian teaching will gradually permeate the planet until peace reigns. No, Paul says that there will be a cataclysmic supernatural intervention by God that will put a stop to a regime of maximal evil. The question is: How do we know whether this apocalyptic scenario is true or not?

Paul says that one of the ways in which the Thessalonians could know that this would happen is that the seeds of the thinking that would lead to it were already visible in the Roman culture of the day: "For the mystery of lawlessness is already at work" (2 Thessalonians 2:7). Paul clearly does not mean lawlessness in the sense of the absence of civil law – Rome was famous for its laws, and to this day, some of those laws form the basis of European law. Paul, as the context shows, is talking about *spiritual* lawlessness, the blasphemy of human beings who claim divinity, as many kings in the past had done and as some of the Roman emperors were already doing at the time. Christians who refused to acknowledge this were often persecuted and killed.

We have already seen that the idea of *Homo deus* is rooted in Genesis. That, however, is only the beginning of the narrative of the human endeavour to play God or to be God. From time to time in the Old Testament record it rears its head – we read of emperors like the Babylonian Nebuchadnezzar (Daniel 3) and the Greek Antiochus Epiphanes (Daniel 11:21–32), who arrogated divine powers to themselves, the latter using those powers to justify violence.

The ruling Roman emperors assumed divine honours. For example, Julius Caesar was regarded as a god – Divus Julius – and in later New Testament times, that element in the Imperial Cult led to periods of persecution for Christians who bravely paid with their lives for refusing to bow down and worship the emperor as a *Homo deus*.

At every turn, it would seem, humanity's efforts to achieve divinity have been associated with an overweening arrogance and a sense of superiority that, far from achieving something superhuman, has produced something terrifyingly subhuman and bestial. The more they try to elevate themselves, the more they sink into a morass of violence and tyranny, as was horrifically demonstrated in the twentieth century. Hannah Arendt, who wrote one of the first books on totalitarianism – *The Origins of Totalitarianism* (published in 1951) – was convinced that totalitarianism was rooted in a utopianism based on the rejection of God and the deification of man. She wrote perceptively:

> What binds these men together is a firm and sincere belief in human omnipotence. Their moral cynicism, their belief that everything is permitted, rests on the solid conviction that everything is possible . . . In trying to create a perverse heaven on earth, totalitarian systems acknowledge no limit on either their conduct or their aspirations. They take Dostoyevsky's chilling warning that "if God does not exist, everything is permitted" and institutionalise it in the Party. From there it is but a short distance to the mass killing and terror endemic to totalitarianism – from Nazi Germany's Auschwitz and Treblinka, to the Soviet Union's Lubyanka prison and Perm-36 gulag, to Communist China's Great Leap Forward and Cultural Revolution . . . The concentration and extermination camps of totalitarian regimes serve as the laboratories in which the fundamental belief of totalitarianism that everything is possible is being verified.[10]

According to Paul, the same dark shadow looms over the future of humanity. The horrific totalitarian vision Paul outlines in his second letter to the Thessalonian Christians is very likely to be characterised by rigid and oppressive civil laws, but at the spiritual level, it is in its essence lawless rebellion against Almighty God – hence the description, "man of lawlessness." Paul told the Thessalonians that what will happen in the future is the inevitable harvest of the attempt to deify humans that was already visible in their Roman culture at the time.

We should not, therefore, be surprised to see it played out in the future on a global scale. And as we observe developments in China, we shall scarcely be surprised either to see it associated with totalitarian social control. It is, alas, not difficult to imagine that programme being rolled out around the world. The way world politics are going, it's not impossible to think that power will be concentrated into the hands of fewer and fewer people, so that we could well imagine the existence of a world-state in the future that is controlled by a single person with extraordinary authority – a *Homo deus* whose powers of rule and deception are derived from the most sinister of all superhuman intelligences – the devil himself.

It is the fact that the *Homo deus* idea pervades history that makes the biblical scenario more than plausible. Of course, it contradicts the widespread idea that human beings are basically good and are improving all the time so that eventually bad behaviour will be eliminated and one of Max Tegmark's more humane and benevolent scenarios will be more likely to characterise the future – Protector God, Benevolent Dictator, or Egalitarian Utopia.[11] That seems like wishful thinking in light of the biblical material and of the experience of the twentieth century. Interestingly enough, it also seems like wishful thinking in light of Yuval Harari's sobering conclusion to *Sapiens*:

Moreover, despite the astonishing things that humans are capable of doing, we remain unsure of our goals and we seem to be as discontented as ever. We have advanced from canoes to galleys to steamships to space shuttles – but nobody knows where we're going. We are more powerful than ever before, but have very little idea what to do with all that power. Worse still, humans seem to be more irresponsible than ever. Self-made gods with only the laws of physics to keep us company, we are accountable to no one. We are consequently wreaking havoc on our fellow animals and on the surrounding ecosystem, seeking little more than our own comfort and amusement, yet never finding satisfaction.

Is there anything more dangerous than dissatisfied and irresponsible gods who don't know what they want?[12]

NOTES

1. C. S. Lewis, *God in the Dock: Essays on Theology and Ethics* (Grand Rapids: Eerdmans, 2014), 99.

2. David J. Bosch, *Transforming Mission: Paradigm Shifts in Theology of Mission* (Maryknoll, NY: Orbis, 2011), 328.

3. Stephen Pinker, *The Better Angels of Our Nature: Why Violence Has Declined* (New York: Penguin, 2012).

4. John Gray, "Best of 2012: Stephen Pinker's Delusions of Peace," *ABC Religion & Ethics*, 20 January 2013, www.abc.net.au/religion/best-of-2012 -stephen-pinkers-delusions-of-peace/10100056.

5. From the Greek *ou* = "not" and *topos* = "place." The homophone *Eutopia* (Greek *Eu* = "good") means a "good place," and the two are often confused. In 1872, Samuel Butler published his novel, a satire on Victorian society, called *Erewhon*, which is (almost) "nowhere" spelt backwards. The fictional country Erewhon at first appears to be a Utopia, but that turns out not to be the case.

6. We should notice how often the clouds of heaven are mentioned in connection with Christ's return – it is to be a literal and visible coming.

7. Many people find the idea of vicarious suffering difficult. I have written about it in *Gunning for God* (Oxford: Lion, 2011), 145–64.

8. There is discussion here: if such an upload were ever to be possible, would the result be recognisably me? See David J. Chalmers, *The Character of Consciousness* (Oxford: Oxford University Press, 2010).

9. John Gray, *Seven Types of Atheism* (New York: Farrar, Straus and Giroux, 2018), 70.

10. Hannah Arendt, *The Origins of Totalitarianism* (1951; repr., London: Penguin, 2017), 387, 437.

11. See "Summary of 12 AI Aftermath Scenarios," Future of Life Institute, https://futureoflife.org/ai-aftermath-scenarios.

12. Yuval Noah Harari, *Sapiens* (New York: HarperCollins, 2015), 415–16.

CHAPTER TWELVE

HOMO DEUS IN THE BOOK OF REVELATION

The last book of the New Testament, written the best part of 2,000 years ago, describes a future *Homo deus* that embodies the features both of Paul's "man of lawlessness" and Tegmark's Prometheus. In the visions of Revelation 12–13, we are introduced to the extremely vivid spectacle of a horrific beast with seven heads and ten horns to whom the devil Satan (pictured both as a snake and a dragon) gives immense power and worldwide authority. This beast becomes a blasphemous object of worship for the entire world, as does the devil that empowers it.

We immediately recognise multiple parallels with the description of the man of lawlessness in 2 Thessalonians, so that Revelation backs up in imagery and metaphor what Paul says in plain prose. For metaphor, as C. S. Lewis is at pains to point out, is always used to stand for something real, not for something unreal. Saying "my heart is broken," is using a metaphor to describe a very real, painful emotional experience, not something imaginary.

Here in Revelation, the metaphor of a beast is evidently

used to describe a very real hostile state, as anyone with even a rudimentary knowledge of the biblical narrative would have no difficulty in recognising. After all, centuries earlier, the prophet Daniel had used the imagery of wild beasts to describe various kinds of empires and their leaders. And the first readers of the book of Revelation would have had no difficulty recognising a state that behaved like a beast, since they actually lived in one – the Roman Empire. They got the message loud and clear, and any reader who took it seriously would realise that, although the imagery applied to certain aspects of the behaviour of the Roman Empire, there was, as we shall see, a further – and highly plausible – deeper application to the state of the world in the future leading up to the return of Christ.

Therefore, before dismissing these visions as apocalyptic fantasy, readers should pay careful attention to the following excerpt from the book of Revelation in order to be able to make an informed attempt to use their imagination to understand what the imagery is intended to convey:

> And I saw a beast rising out of the sea, with ten horns and seven heads, with ten diadems on its horns and blasphemous names on its heads. And the beast that I saw was like a leopard; its feet were like a bear's, and its mouth was like a lion's mouth. And to it the dragon gave his power and his throne and great authority. One of its heads seemed to have a mortal wound, but its mortal wound was healed, and the whole earth marveled as they followed the beast. And they worshiped the dragon, for he had given his authority to the beast, and they worshiped the beast, saying, "Who is like the beast, and who can fight against it?"

And the beast was given a mouth uttering haughty and blasphemous words, and it was allowed to exercise authority for forty-two months. It opened its mouth to utter blasphemies against God, blaspheming his name and his dwelling, that is, those who dwell in heaven. Also it was allowed to make war on the saints and to conquer them. And authority was given it over every tribe and people and language and nation, and all who dwell on earth will worship it, everyone whose name has not been written before the foundation of the world in the book of life of the Lamb who was slain.

Revelation 13:1–8

We note immediately the marked similarities between this description of the beast and that of the anti-God man of lawlessness in 2 Thessalonians. We also see that the global, violently maintained authority of this "beast" is established through the healing of a "mortal wound" in one of its heads. Although we cannot say precisely what this refers to, it sounds like a parody of the central events of the death and resurrection of Christ that establish his authority as Messiah and Son of God.

We note also that although this horrific beast is permitted to lay waste to the Christian community, its tenure of power is strictly limited. The scenario is now made more complex with the arrival of another "beast":

Then I saw another beast rising out of the earth. It had two horns like a lamb and it spoke like a dragon. It exercises all the authority of the first beast in its presence and makes the earth and its inhabitants worship the first beast, whose mortal wound was healed. It performs great signs, even making fire come down from heaven to earth in front of people, and by the signs that it is allowed to work in the presence of the beast it deceives those who dwell on earth, telling them to make an image for the beast that was wounded by the sword and yet lived. And it was allowed to give breath to the image of the beast, so that the image of the beast might even speak and might cause those who would not worship the image of the beast to be slain. Also it causes all, both small and great, both rich and poor, both free and slave, to be marked on the right hand or the forehead, so that no one can buy or sell unless he has the mark, that is, the name of the beast or the number of its name. This calls for wisdom: let the one who has understanding calculate the number of the beast, for it is the number of a man, and his number is 666.

Revelation 13:11–18

Revelation 13:15 describes this second beast as commanding the construction of an image of the first beast to which breath is given – resulting in worldwide deception and control. All who refuse to bow down and acknowledge the authority of the beast are killed. Social control is absolute, as freedom to buy and sell is determined by the wearing of some kind of mark – an implanted chip, or Tegmark's bracelet or similar, that will determine whether or not a person is regarded as socially acceptable – analogous to having a certain number of social security points in the evolving Chinese algorithmic surveillance system.

In this connection, one naturally thinks of AGI proponents' aim to make artificial life and to upload the contents of minds onto silicon. While we do not know exactly what Revelation has in mind here, it could conceivably be the creation of some kind of "life" that is so sophisticated and impressive that the world is deceived and oppressed by it. That is, it could represent some partial realisation of AGI. Of course, the use of the word *image* should not necessarily conjure up in our minds some kind of primitive stone or wooden image. At every stage of history, human beings have set up images and bowed down to worship the creations of their own hands and minds and have dreamed of somehow giving life to their creations – as in the Jewish folklore story of the creation of Golem from inanimate matter. Perhaps, in some sense, they one day will.

It is important to point out that idols were, and still are, things that people trusted rather than things they loved. They often feared their idols. "Worship" meant more an acceptance of superior authority, a "bowing down" before that authority, rather than carrying any sense of affection or positive devotion. Throughout Old Testament history, up to the exile in Babylon, the people of Israel were constantly compromising with the idolatrous practices of their pagan neighbours, and the prophets constantly reminded them of the tragic absurdity of such compromise. Here is one of the most famous sayings of the prophet Isaiah on the topic as he mocks the naivete of the ancient idol-maker fashioning a wooden god from a tree that he has just felled:

> Half of the wood he burns in the fire;
> over it he prepares his meal,

he roasts his meat and eats his fill.
He also warms himself and says,
    "Ah! I am warm; I see the fire."
From the rest he makes a god, his idol;
    he bows down to it and worships.
He prays to it and says,
    "Save me! You are my god!"

Isaiah 44:16–17 NIV

Isaiah piles on the sarcasm – the absurdity of making a god, whether of iron or wood, the incredible blindness of taking wood and using one part of it to make a cooking fire and shaping the other part into a human form and bowing down to it. The Psalms also point out that, although the image may have human form, it is useless because it cannot reproduce any human function:

The idols of the nations are silver and gold,
    made by human hands.
They have mouths, but cannot speak,
    eyes, but cannot see.
They have ears, but cannot hear,
    nor is there breath in their mouths.
Those who make them will be like them,
    and so will all who trust in them.

Psalm 135:15–18 NIV

It is clear that the book of Revelation is talking about something very different from this kind of crude idolatry when it describes an image to which breath and speech is given.

This seems much more "human" than ancient primitive images, and it could well suggest something like a brilliantly contrived humanoid robot equipped with very advanced AI, even AGI. The fact that the whole earth worships the beast because of the image is no trivial embellishment. To get the attention of the whole world would be an unprecedented achievement – sadly rendered credible by the existence of global visual communication networks on the internet and television.

This scenario inevitably raises the question: How far will God permit humans to go? According to the biblical narrative, God intervened in the first *Homo deus* project in Genesis 3. He intervened once more in the later one at Babel, where humans made a concerted attempt to use their intellectual and technological skills to construct a tower that would reach to heaven – another symptom of the egoism that fuels *Homo deus*. According to the biblical narrative, God will intervene in the future to bring human rebellion to an end. However, is it just as possible nevertheless that he will not intervene at the point where we might most expect it on the basis of the previous interventions just mentioned?

What gives rise to that possibility is the fact that Revelation 13 places considerable emphasis on what the various beasts are *allowed* to do. This is in line with the theological teaching that God is ultimately in control and nothing happens outside his permissive will.[1] The first beast is *allowed* to exercise authority for forty-two months and *allowed* to make war on the saints and to conquer them. The second beast is *allowed* to perform deceiving signs. Also, it is *allowed* to give breath to the image of the beast.

The language here is reminiscent of that used in Genesis:

"Then the LORD God formed the man of dust from the ground and breathed into his nostrils the breath of life, and the man became a living creature" (Genesis 2:7). Does this indicate that humans will be allowed to create something very lifelike, if not some sort of life itself? If that is the case, the danger is that if we are wrongly convinced that God will intervene before such a stage is reached, the deception for us when it happens may be even greater.

We note further that this "living" image is able to cause the selective death of those who do not worship the beast. That implies that, whatever it is, it is able to recognise such "recalcitrant, anti-social behaviour" (facial recognition?), determine their attitude towards the beast (social surveillance?), and put them, or have them put, to death. All of these are very complex processes to implement globally. So does this imply AGI at a level that can simulate a kind of consciousness, or is it an upgraded version of the (unconscious) type of AI systems used today?

If so, this text in Revelation represents a timely warning to all earth-dwellers that is of particular relevance to this technologically advanced generation and to those who follow it. It would be a serious, if not fatal, mistake if, having read this biblical scenario, we think we are dealing with childish fantasies that are easily recognised and exposed. We are not. We are dealing with the possibility of an all-too-real global tyranny with social control at its heart, a totalitarian surveillance state as envisaged in Tegmark's Prometheus scenario that is eerily like the one under active development and testing in China today. What is obvious and very disturbing is that people readily "worship" such systems – that is, they bow down to them and accept their authority, sacrificing their freedom in the interests of supposed security. Indeed, in a sense we are all doing this by incrementally handing over our decisions to AI and letting it increasingly determine many aspects of our everyday lives.

We now ask: What does the beast in Revelation 13 stand for? In a general sense, the answer is not difficult, since this beast is said to have control of the world economy. It causes everyone to be marked on the right hand or forehead so that no one can buy or sell unless they have the mark that is the name of the beast or the number of its name (think of the Prometheus security bracelet). But does it represent a collective body like a world government or a state that behaves in a bestial way, or does it represent an individual? The text itself indicates that the beast is an individual – indeed, a *human* individual. Revelation 13:18 says: "let the one who has understanding calculate the number of the beast, for it is the number of a man, and his number is 666."

A great deal of attention – indeed far too much attention – has been paid to the number 666 that appears here. It is evidently a *gematria*.[2] There has been endless guessing as to who this powerful leader will be. Such speculation seems to be self-evidently fruitless. If we have to guess who is intended, we are going to be wrong, since the context has already informed us that the "man of lawlessness" will be revealed by Satanic power. When this world power appears, there will be no need to guess who it is.

Decoding the gematria 666 will be a simple retrospective check, not a profound puzzle. For this passage is not concerned with answering the question of *who* the beast is, but rather, as is explicitly stated, *what* it is. It is, says John, "the number of a man." That is, the beast is a symbol; the reality behind that symbol is *a man*. The beast that is energised by the serpent is a human being who claims deity and thus fits the description *Homo deus*. The rebellion against God that started in Genesis will therefore reach a climax in a fearful *Homo deus* project about which Harari, among others, seems to know nothing.

We deduce that it makes sense to think that both 2 Thessalonians and Revelation speak of the same devil-inspired, anti-god, immensely powerful world leader who will in a future time claim divine honours and deceive the world by false wonders and who will be cataclysmically destroyed by the return of Christ in power and great glory. Here is the description of that momentous event as depicted in Revelation:

> Then I saw heaven opened, and behold, a white horse! The one sitting on it is called Faithful and True, and in righteousness he judges and makes war. His eyes are like a flame of fire, and on his head are many diadems, and he has a name written that no one knows but himself. He is clothed in a robe dipped in blood, and the name by which he is called is The Word of God. And the armies of heaven, arrayed in fine linen, white and pure, were following him on white horses. From his mouth comes a sharp sword with which to strike down the nations, and he will rule them with a rod of iron. He will tread the winepress of the fury of the wrath of God the Almighty. On his robe and on his thigh he has a name written, King of kings and Lord of lords . . .

And I saw the beast and the kings of the earth with their armies gathered to make war against him who was sitting on the horse and against his army. And the beast was captured, and with it the false prophet who in its presence had done the signs by which he deceived those who had received the mark of the beast and those who worshiped its image. These two were thrown alive into the lake of fire that burns with sulfur.

Revelation 19:11–16, 19–20

A REMARKABLE FUTURE SCENARIO PREDICTED IN AN ANCIENT VISION

In order to get more perspective on this, we recall that the imagery used in the book of Revelation is rooted in chapter 7 of the book of Daniel. I would ask the reader before proceeding any further to read that chapter in its entirety to get the breadth of Daniel's vision.

Collecting together some of the main points from this vision, we see:

- There is an immensely powerful beast (the fourth beast) with ten horns, and a little horn that speaks great words.
- The beast makes war with the saints and prevails.
- The Son of Man comes on the clouds of heaven.
- The heavenly court passes judgment on the beast and destroys it.
- The saints receive the kingdom.

Note the many features that Daniel's beast has in common with Revelation's beast:

- It has ten horns that are said to be ten kings (Daniel 7:24, cf. Revelation 17:12).
- It utters haughty words.
- It makes war with the saints and prevails.
- Its authority is limited – Daniel: "time, times, and half a time," (7:25), that is, three and a half times; Revelation: "42 months" (13:5), that is, three and a half years.
- The beast in Revelation combines features of the first three beasts in Daniel's vision: it was like a leopard, its feet like a bear's, and its mouth like a lion's (Revelation 13:2).

The similarities are remarkable. Furthermore, the beast in Daniel is judged in the context of the coming of the Son of Man on the clouds of heaven. The beast in Revelation is destroyed by the coming from heaven to earth of the Rider on the White Horse, who is said to be the Word of God, King of kings, and Lord of lords.[3] It is surely not fanciful to suggest that Daniel and Revelation are describing the same thing, in very similar, highly symbolic language – and what they are describing is laid out for us, as we have seen, in the plain, non-symbolic language of 2 Thessalonians 2, where Paul is writing about the destruction of the man of lawlessness by the coming of Christ.

Playing God has always been a temptation for powerful leaders. As we have seen, Paul pointed out in his day that "the mystery of lawlessness is already at work" (2 Thessalonians 2:7).

Paul was referring to spiritual lawlessness: that defiance of God that characterised the Roman emperors (and many before them), who thought of themselves as gods and demanded that they should be worshiped. This resonates with a further detail in the description of the fourth beast in Daniel 7: "[He] shall think to change the times and the law; and they shall be given into his hand for a time, times, and half a time" (Daniel 7:25). Daniel had already experienced a clash between the law of his God and a law of the state that had been crafted by evil power brokers who wanted to get rid of him (Daniel 6).

This vision says that Daniel's experience on that occasion will not be the last of its kind. Indeed, worse is to come. Darius forbade worship of God for a month. Under the fourth beast, the ban will last for much longer – three and a half *times*, usually understood to mean three and a half years. What is more, this beast will think to "change the times," that is, the set times of the feasts and ceremonies that the nation of Israel celebrates as part of their worship of God.

Hence, the fourth beast can be seen as the final manifestation of human rebellion against God. Both 2 Thessalonians and Revelation point out that the divinity-claiming man-beast is energised by the dark power of Satan and is a master of deception. In keeping with the progressive nature of biblical prophetic revelation, this information is not contained in Daniel's description. In fact, the account in Revelation is more detailed than Daniel's in several other respects. It tells us additionally that the beast had seven heads, and it introduces a second beast that "exercises all the authority of the first beast in its presence, and makes the earth and its inhabitants worship the first beast . . . It deceives those who dwell on earth" (Revelation

13:12, 14). We are also told: "the ten horns . . . are ten kings who have not yet received royal power, but they are to receive authority as kings for one hour, together with the beast. These are of one mind, and they hand over their power and authority to the beast. They will make war on the Lamb, and the Lamb will conquer them" (Revelation 17:12–14).

Just as we found with the prophecy of the seed (Genesis 3:15), the nearer we get to the time of fulfilment, the more detail is given to us. If we put it all together, a picture emerges of an extraordinary political arrangement in which ten kings or leaders cede their authority to a leader of immense power and authority. The implication is that, whoever these ten leaders are, they exist simultaneously, and either voluntarily or forcibly, they hand over the reins of their power to a single dictator – the man of lawlessness. Since he appears to hold power over the entire planet, what is envisaged here is nothing less than a world government.[4]

WORLD GOVERNMENT?

We have never yet seen anything like this in history, but it is far from being a wild and irrational idea. In recent times, nations have felt the need to form international organisations, like the United Nations, in order to help maintain a balance of power, police the world, and keep the peace. However, the UN has had a mixed record, and some very influential leaders have suggested, and still do, that the only real solution to the world's political and social problems is an international government. In the aftermath of World War II, Albert Einstein wrote: "A world government must be created which is able to solve conflicts between nations by judicial decision. This government must be based on a clearcut constitution which is approved by the governments and nations and which gives it the sole disposition of offensive weapons."[5]

In today's globalised world, a world government is an entirely plausible notion. We have courts of international law, and in Europe we are all aware of a steady creep towards less and less independence and more and more centralized control. For many, that seems to pave the way towards a United States of Europe. In the *Financial Times* on 8 December 2008, Gideon Rachman wrote: "I have never believed that there is a secret United Nations plot to take over the US. I have never seen black helicopters hovering in the sky above Montana. But, for the first time in my life, I think the formation of some sort of world government is plausible."[6]

A world government would involve much more than co-operation between nations. It would be an entity with state-like characteristics, backed by a body of laws. The European Union has already set up a continental government for twenty-seven countries, which could be a model. The EU has a supreme court, a currency, thousands of pages of legislation, a large civil service, and the ability to deploy military force – and the desire to build one.

Could the European model go global? There are three reasons for thinking that it might. Firstly, it is increasingly clear that the most difficult issues facing national governments are international in nature: there is global warming, a global financial crisis, and a "global war on terror."

Secondly, it could be done. The transport and communications revolutions have shrunk the world so that, as Geoffrey

Blainey, an eminent Australian historian wrote, "For the first time in human history, world government of some sort is now possible."[7] Mr. Blainey foresaw an attempt to form a world government at some point in the next two centuries, which is an unusually long time-horizon for the average newspaper column.

But – the third point – a change in the political atmosphere suggests that global governance could come much sooner than that. The financial crisis and climate change have been pushing national governments towards global solutions, even in countries such as China and the United States that are traditionally fierce guardians of national sovereignty. Jacques Attali, an adviser to President Nicolas Sarkozy of France, argued: "Global governance is just a euphemism for global government." As far as he is concerned, some form of global government cannot come too soon. Mr. Attali believed that the "core of the international financial crisis is that we have global financial markets and no global rule of law."[8] It seems, then, that everything is in place. For the first time since *Homo sapiens* began to doodle on cave walls, there is an argument, an opportunity, and a means to make serious steps towards a world government.

The idea of a world government has been around for a long time. It refers to the idea of all humankind united under one common political authority. Arguably, it has not existed so far in human history, yet proposals for a unified global political authority have existed since ancient times – in the ambition of kings, popes, and emperors and in the dreams of poets and philosophers.

For instance, in the Middle Ages the Italian poet, philosopher, and statesman Dante Alighieri (1265–1321) argued it was possible to eliminate war if "the whole earth, and all that is given to the human race to possess, should be a Monarchy – that is, a single principality, having one prince who, possessing all things and being unable to desire anything else, would keep the kings content within the boundaries of their kingdoms and preserve among them the peace in which the cities might rest."[9]

The German philosopher Immanuel Kant held that reason suggested the formation of "an *international state (civitas gentium)*, which would necessarily continue to grow until it embraced all the peoples of the earth."[10] Yet Kant had strong reservations about a world monarchy. He thought that a federal union of free and independent states "is still to be preferred to an amalgamation of the separate nations under a single power which has overruled the rest and created a universal monarchy." His reason for hesitation was: "For the laws progressively lose their impact as the government increases its range, and a soulless despotism, after crushing the germs of goodness, will finally lapse into anarchy." Kant thought that a "universal despotism" would end "in the graveyard of freedom."[11]

NOTES

1. For more on this complex topic, see my *Determined to Believe?* (Oxford: Lion, 2017).

2. A number that is formed by adding together the numbers representing the letters of the name according to some agreed-on scheme – for example, A = 1, B = 2, etc. For instance, a boy in the ancient world might carve on a tree: "I love the girl whose number is 53," and would leave others to work out, by a trial and error process of substituting letters for numbers, that her name was Julia.

3. Some scholars understand the Son of Man "coming on the clouds of heaven" (Matthew 26:64) as a reference to the ascension of Christ, when he came to God and his throne. However, I think: (1) our Lord's citation of this text at his trial is more naturally understood in terms of his future return to earth, and thus being visible

to those who have rejected him, and (2) if Daniel 7 is referring to the ascension, it is fair to ask: Did God's judgment occur at the ascension? And if so, what beast was then destroyed? See my book *Against the Flow: The Inspiration of Daniel in an Age of Relativism* (Oxford: Monarch, 2015) on the issue.

4. Hence the identification in earlier years with ten European countries was wide off the mark.

5. Albert Einstein, "Towards a World Government" (1946), in *Out of My Later Years* (New York: Philosophical Library, 1956), 146.

6. Gideon Rachman, "And Now for a World Government," *Financial Times*, 8 December 2008, www.ft.com/content/7a03e5b6-c541-11dd-b516-000077b07658.

7. Quoted in Rachman, "And Now for a World Government."

8. Quoted in Rachman, "And Now for a World Government."

9. Dante Alighieri, *Il Convivio* (*The Banquet*), book 4, chapter 4, trans. Richard H. Lansing (Garland Library of Medieval Literature, 1990), https://digitaldante .columbia.edu/text/library/the-convivio/book-04/#30.

10. Immanuel Kant, *Perpetual Peace* (1795), 105, cited in Catherine Lu, "World Government," in *The Stanford Encyclopedia of Philosophy*, ed. Edward N. Zalta (Winter 2016), https://plato.stanford.edu/archives/win2016/entries/world-govern ment, italics original.

11. Kant, *Perpetual Peace*, 113, 114; cited in Lu, "World Government."

CHAPTER THIRTEEN

THE TIME OF THE END

Comparing Daniel, Revelation, and 2 Thessalonians, the oppression of the fierce fourth beast, the man of lawlessness, sounds very much like Immanuel Kant's "graveyard of freedom" mentioned at the end of the previous chapter. It is for this reason that the message of Daniel 7 is of great importance. It would appear that Daniel is saying that the final form of government will be a world government of hideous strength, overtly and maximally hostile towards God.

What is very interesting is that in the biblical books just mentioned; in the famous dystopias like *We*, *Brave New World*, *1984*; and in many of the contemporary scenarios, absolute power is eventually concentrated into the hands of one man – a beast in Daniel, the beast in Revelation, the man of lawlessness in Thessalonians, the Well-Doer in *We*, the Big Brother in *1984*, the Head in *That Hideous Strength*, Prometheus in Tegmark, and so forth. In *Brave New World*, there are ten World Controllers, of which only one, Mustapha Mond, figures in the novel.

C. S. Lewis gives a possible reason for this in his novel *That Hideous Strength*. Mark Studdock, a rather gullible and ambitious academic, is informed by a senior person, another academic, Filostrato, that the sinister scientific institute, N.I.C.E., for which he works, has managed to keep alive the brain of a dead person and now possesses the power to deliver physical immortality.

"At first, of course," said Filostrato, "the power will be confined to a number – a small number – of individual men. Those who are selected for eternal life."

"And you mean," said Mark, "it will then be extended to all men?"

"No," said Filostrato, "I mean it will then be reduced to one man. You are not a fool, are you, my young friend? All that talk about the power of Man over Nature – Man in the abstract – is only for the *canaglia*.[1] You know as well as I do that Man's power over Nature is only the power of some men over other men with Nature as the instrument.[2] There is no such thing as Man – it is a word. There are only men. No! It is not Man who will be omnipotent. It is some one man, some immortal man."[3]

At this point, a renegade cleric, Straik, joins the conversation:

"God will have power to give eternal reward and eternal punishment."

"God?" said Mark. "How does He come into it? I don't believe in God."

"But, my friend," said Filostrato, "does it follow that because there was no God in the past that there will be no God also in the future?"

"Don't you see," said Straik, "that we are offering you the unspeakable glory of being present at the creation of God Almighty? Here, in this house, you shall meet the first sketch of the real God. It is a man – or a being made by man – who will finally ascend the throne of the universe. And rule forever."[4]

HARARI'S *HOMO DEUS* ANTICIPATED?

It would appear that the drive towards the deification of human beings inevitably leads to the eventual concentration of power in the hands of one "superman" who effectively enslaves the rest. The secular dystopias serve to enhance the credibility of the biblical one.

I would reiterate that I have no intention of attempting to identify the final world-state or when it will emerge, let alone who will be its leader. I do not know, and we are not there yet. In any case, as I mentioned above, when the time comes, there will be no need to speculate: it will be only too obvious. Why, then, should we even bother thinking about such details? For all we know, these events may well be in the far distant future, so how can they be relevant to us?

There are at least two answers to that. Firstly, when Paul wrote, these events were twenty centuries more distant than they are now. Yet Paul thought it was important even then to tell the Christians in Thessalonica about the man of lawlessness. He gives the reason: "for the mystery of lawlessness is already at work" (2 Thessalonians 2:7). That is, the kind of *Homo deus* thinking that would eventually dominate the world was already foreshadowed in what was happening at the time in Roman society.

Paul warns that we should pay close attention to such trends in history. They are not innocent. They will lead inexorably to the greatest state-orchestrated hostility to God that the world has ever seen. Genesis tells us that the war against God started a long time ago, at the very dawn of human history. But in the Western world, we have lived to see a ramping-up of open hostility not only to God but also to public expression of belief in him.

One major negative effect of the Enlightenment was the propagation of the idea that all true knowledge is factual, value-free, and objective. By contrast with facts, values were held to be subjective, essentially a matter of taste. The conviction then grew that religious belief belonged to the realm of private values rather than public truth. Link that with the increasing notion that human beings are autonomous and emancipated, and you have a potent recipe for banishing God.

Nowadays, the scathing New Atheist demagogues announce that science, with its reliance on reason and evidence, leaves no room for belief in God, since, as they falsely assume, faith in him has no evidential basis. The way is open, at least in theory, for prominent figures in a predominantly godless society to construct an AGI to implement their own atheistic agenda.

With what I can only describe as culpable short-sightedness, the (now not so) New Atheists stir up needless hostility by accusing Christianity of a great deal of cruelty and violence. In making such accusations, they fail to take into account what they surely must know: (1) that Jesus himself forbade violence in his name, and (2) that the worst violence in history is to be seen in the mass murders perpetrated by atheist regimes in the twentieth century.[5] Thinking of that always reminds me of what a Russian intellectual said to me in the 1990s: "We thought we could get rid of God and retain a value for human beings, but we found out too late that it was impossible to do so." What value social surveillance AI or AGI will leave for human beings who fall foul of the system and what wars might be generated in the struggle for technological dominance are yet other questions to be answered.

In his prophecy, Daniel shows us that the attempt to eliminate God will eventually lead, not to freedom, but to intense oppression. Atheists like Friedrich Nietzsche saw this clearly: the "death" of God would not lead to human freedom but to nihilism and the loss of everything, including meaning. These issues need to be brought again into public discourse in the light of what AI is already capable of doing.

I have already pointed out the danger of thinking that the kingdom of God on earth would eventually be brought about by Christian teaching permeating society in such a way that the world and its governmental structures would become Christian. The biblical "map" says the very opposite – the kingdom of God in its outward sense will arrive with the supernatural return of Christ to bring the global tyranny of "the beast" to its deserved end.

Surely, someone will say, *we can prepare ourselves for this kind of thing, can't we, without all the bizarre details about horns and heads?* Well, firstly, the vivid imagery is meant to convey an impression of very important realities – horns, a symbol of power, for instance, and heads, of rule and intellect. Secondly, some of the AGI scenarios are equally or even more bizarre.

But leaving that aside, there is a second reason for such

predictions in Scripture. The apostle John describes how Jesus drove the money changers out of the temple at Passover time in Jerusalem:

> So the Jews said to him, "What sign do you show us for doing these things?" Jesus answered them, "Destroy this temple, and in three days I will raise it up." The Jews then said, "It has taken forty-six years to build this temple, and will you raise it up in three days?" But he was speaking about the temple of his body. When therefore he was raised from the dead, his disciples remembered that he had said this, and they believed the Scripture and the word that Jesus had spoken.
>
> *John 2:18–22*

At the time Jesus made this prediction, his disciples could make no sense of it. But when the actual event occurred some time later, they remembered it, and it strengthened their faith in him. Just before the crucifixion, in order to comfort his disciples, Jesus told them he was going away and then explained why: "And now I have told you before it takes place, so that when it does take place you may believe" (John 14:29).

These two examples from John's Gospel refer to specific events. The import of the predictions was only realised at the time of the events themselves – not before. Therefore, one would expect that some of the details in Daniel, Thessalonians, and Revelation will only be understood at the time of their fulfilment. Daniel expressly states that some of his prophecy will be sealed (that is, will not be understood) until the time of the end (Daniel 12:4). So we cannot expect to understand all the details – a consideration that should help us keep a balance between taking the prophecies and their details seriously and grasping their general outline without indulging in wild speculation.

GROUNDS FOR ULTIMATE HOPE

Over the centuries, Daniel 7 has been a source of real hope to millions of people who have experienced persecution and suffering because of their faith in God. However powerful the beasts may be, when they have done their worst, they can only kill the body, but Jesus himself said that they cannot destroy the person who is you:

> "And do not fear those who kill the body but cannot kill the soul. Rather fear him who can destroy both soul and body in hell. Are not two sparrows sold for a penny? And not one of them will fall to the ground apart from your Father. But even the hairs of your head are all numbered. Fear not, therefore; you are of more value than many sparrows. So everyone who acknowledges me before men, I also will acknowledge before my Father who is in heaven, but whoever denies me before men, I also will deny before my Father who is in heaven."
>
> *Matthew 10:28–33*

The consistent message of Scripture is that there is another world from which the true *Homo Deus* – Jesus Christ the Son of Man who is the Son of God – will one day come. As a perfect human, he will take the reins of government from the beasts of earth. There will be a judgment, where righteous justice will be done and seen to be done. The final ferocious expression of hostility towards God and his people will be destroyed, and those who have clung to God in spite of overwhelming odds – even martyrdom – will receive the kingdom.

At the end of his powerful vision, Daniel records his honest reaction: "My thoughts greatly alarmed me, and my color changed, but I kept the matter in my heart" (Daniel 7:28). It was a disturbing vision that affected him deeply. However strong and deep our faith, however real our experience of God, we are still human beings beset with frailty, and we simply cannot think about the issues this vision raises without being shaken – even if we possess the faith of a man like Daniel.

Daniel kept the vision in his heart and pondered the questions that arose from it for him. So also should we, for we too have our questions. And we will inevitably be challenged: How can we be so sure of the future? What about when those of us who are Christians find ourselves to be a minority facing AI surveillance, invasive social control, and possibly brutal antagonism because of our faith in God? Let us listen to the advice given by the Christian apostle Paul to his young friend and fellow worker Timothy: "Remember Jesus Christ, risen from the dead, the offspring of David, as preached in my gospel, for which I am suffering, bound with chains as a criminal. But the word of God is not bound!" (2 Timothy 2:8–9).

"Remember Jesus Christ, risen from the dead . . ." This is the key to real hope. Death is not the end: it is a fact of history that Jesus rose from the dead. Years earlier, Paul had told the thinkers at Athens that the resurrection of Jesus was the supreme evidence that Jesus would be the Judge in that coming day: "The times of ignorance God overlooked, but now he commands all people everywhere to repent, because he has fixed a day on which he will judge the world in righteousness by a man whom he has appointed; and of this he has given assurance to all by raising him from the dead" (Acts 17:30–31).

The Day of Judgment has been fixed. The evidence is there for all to consider.[6] The designated Judge, the Lord Jesus Christ, has risen from the dead. In that certainty, Paul's confidence was unbounded to the last as he prepared for his final battle with the "beast" of his day:

> For I am already being poured out as a drink offering, and the time of my departure has come. I have fought the good fight, I have finished the race, I have kept the faith. Henceforth there is laid up for me the crown of righteousness, which the Lord, the righteous judge, will award to me on that Day, and not only to me but also to all who have loved his appearing.
>
> *2 Timothy 4:6–8*

CONCLUSION

The teaching of the New Testament about the future brings us face to face with some major issues. So also do some of the scenarios predicted for AGI. How should we react to them? This is an important question. There have been people throughout history who have felt that the only way to respond to the evil embedded in the governmental or commercial structures of this world is to withdraw into a private ghetto or monastery, or to attempt violent overthrow.

Even though he was deeply distressed by the vision, Daniel did not react by withdrawal or violence. He continued to serve the emperor of Babylon and survived to serve at the top level in the succeeding Medo-Persian empire. The New Testament presents us with the same balance. Writing at the time of Nero, Paul says that, on the one hand, the authorities are instituted by God; they are a terror not to good conduct but to bad, and we should respect them (Romans 13:1–7). On the other hand, as we saw above, Paul did not hesitate to say that the "mystery" that would lead to the man of lawlessness was already operating in the very same Roman society (2 Thessalonians 2:7).

Paul is utterly realistic when it comes to the evil endemic both in government structures and in the human heart and the harvest to which it will eventually lead. Yet he does not urge believers to withdraw from the world but encourages them to live productive lives in society as model citizens and Christian witnesses. Fear of AGI should not prevent believers from making a contribution to the positive aspects of narrow AI to the benefit of all.

One outstanding example of this is the work of Rosalind Picard at MIT. She says that the aims of artificial intelligence research have evolved subtly but profoundly. Picard's lab works on creating tools that help computers understand human emotions rather than try to imitate them. She says: "We've decided it's more about building a better human-machine combination than it is about building a machine where we will be lucky if it wants us around as a household pet."[7] Her work has opened up a whole new field called "affective computing," and she has used sophisticated sensors to gain valuable insights into, for instance, the stress levels of autistic children.

And Christians should be involved in getting to grips with the ethical questions that are increasingly being thrown up by both actual and hypothetical technological developments in these fields. One of China's leading pioneers in the AI field, Dr. Kai-Fu Lee, sums up the situation in an interview with Carmine Gallo for *Forbes* on 4 October 2018:

> Dr. Lee realized that AI will not undercut our value as long as we double-down on what makes us truly human. "AI can handle a growing number of non-personal, non-creative routine tasks," Lee told me. But Lee says the skills that make us uniquely human are ones that no machine can replicate. The jobs of the future, says Lee, will require creative, compassionate and empathetic leaders who know how to create trust, build teams, inspire service and communicate effectively.[8]

Such virtues all have to do with the way people think about each other. In this book, we have been thinking – thinking hard – about what people are thinking about possible technological developments. But what about thinking itself? Is it not only important *that* we think but also *how* we think? No account of a Christian assessment of AI would be complete without a (brief) analysis of what the difference is between the thinking behind *Homo deus* projects and the way God thinks and wishes us to think. Man thinks he can become God. But infinitely greater than that is the fact that God thought of becoming human.

Humans, version 1, as originally created by God are (still) unique, and that uniqueness and value is shown by the fact that the central event in history is that God became human. Indeed, one of the most famous biblical passages that describes that event in the context of the grand metanarrative of history was written by Paul in the form of a magnificent poem. Its content analyses the fundamental flaw in the kind of *Homo deus* thinking advocated by Yuval Harari and others. It is an exhortation to model our thinking on that of Christ:

> Have this mind among yourselves, which is yours in Christ Jesus, who, though he was in the form of God, did not count equality with God a thing to be grasped, but emptied himself, by taking the form of a servant, being born in the likeness of men. And being found in human form, he humbled himself by becoming obedient to the point of death, even death on a cross. Therefore God has highly exalted him and bestowed on him the name that is above every name, so that at the name of Jesus every knee should bow, in heaven and on earth and under the earth, and every tongue confess that Jesus Christ is Lord, to the glory of God the Father.
>
> *Philippians 2:5–11*

We have seen that the merely human *Homo deus* projects we have considered originate in *human pride* – the desire not only to be better than other humans but to be like God. Paul condemns this attitude by pointing to the real *Homo Deus*, Jesus Christ, whose lack of pride is demonstrated in that though he was always God and never ceased to be God, "he did not count equality with God a thing to be grasped" (v. 6). This is a clear allusion to Genesis 3, the source of all *Homo deus* fantasies.

Grasping or snatching at godhood is what the first humans did by eating the forbidden fruit. Snatching at godhood is characteristic of transhumanist projects.

But the true *Homo Deus* did not snatch. He did not insist on being treated as God, though God, the eternal Word, he ever was. Rather, he "emptied himself, by taking the form of a servant, being born in the likeness of men" (v. 7). Not only that, but he became "obedient to the point of death, even death on a cross" (v. 8). In so doing, he made a way back to God from the darkness and rebellion of human sin.

The attempt to make a superintelligent *Homo deus* will neither lead back to God nor lead to God, but rather to the greatest rejection of God the world has ever seen. There is no way to a glorious future that bypasses the problem of human sin, and the only one who has offered a viable solution to that problem is Jesus Christ, who faced it head-on on the cross.

And because of that, "God has highly exalted him" (v. 9). The path to true glory and exaltation involved God becoming human in Jesus Christ, who lived, died, rose, and ascended to the world from which he originally came. We are invited to benefit from that staggering sequence of events, but in order to do so, we must first repent of the sinful pride that messed up humanity in the first place, and then we need to entrust our lives to Christ as Saviour and follow him as Lord.

It is this and only this message that can bring real hope to the world, and we who believe it have to be prepared to face a hail of opposition. Daniel and his friends in their day, and Jesus and his apostles in theirs, were prepared to protest against authorities that usurped the place that only God should fill. We shall need all the wisdom from above that God can give us in this AI age in order to fulfil Christ's directive that we should be salt and light in our society.[9] We have often referred to the fact that we live in a surveillance society. Let us therefore live with the myriad cameras and tracers on our lives in such a way that even the monitors can see that we have been with Jesus. After all, whereas "the 'artificial' in artificial intelligence is real,"[10] the divine upgrades are real and not artificial:

- **Phase 1:** "But to all who did receive him, who believed in his name, he gave the right to become children of God" (John 1:12).
- **Phase 2:** "For the trumpet will sound, and the dead will be raised imperishable, and we shall be changed . . . This mortal body must put on immortality" (1 Corinthians 15:52–53).

I am writing these closing words at Christmastime, with the magnificent words of Handel's "Hallelujah Chorus" ringing in my ears: "And He shall reign forever and ever." The Christian narrative will one day come to its fulfilment, as Isaiah the prophet predicted centuries ago:

> For to us a child is born,
>> to us a son is given;
> and the government shall be upon his shoulder,
>> and his name shall be called
> Wonderful Counselor, Mighty God,
>> Everlasting Father, Prince of Peace.
> Of the increase of his government and of peace
>> there will be no end,

on the throne of David and over his kingdom,
 to establish it and to uphold it
with justice and with righteousness
 from this time forth and forevermore.

Isaiah 9:6–7

The wonder is that we can, if we desire, become part of this unending story and live in eternal fellowship with the infinitely intelligent and compassionate Saviour, Jesus Christ the Lord. Nothing artificial can compare with that reality.

NOTES

1. Italian for "scoundrels" or "rabble."

2. The idea expressed here is taken nearly verbatim from C. S. Lewis, *The Abolition of Man* (1943; repr., San Francisco: HarperSanFrancisco, 2001), 55.

3. C. S. Lewis, *That Hideous Strength* (New York: Scribner, 1996), 175.

4. Lewis, *That Hideous Strength*, 176.

5. For more details, see my book *Gunning for God* (Oxford: Lion, 2011).

6. The resurrection of Christ is not offered as evidence for believers only, nor is it "created" by believers' faith. The resurrection, with its consequences, is the historical event that provides the evidence base that justifies faith. Faith, in the Christian sense, is thoroughly evidence-based. It is not blind belief, as is often erroneously suggested.

7. Quoted in Adam Higginbotham, "Welcome to Rosalind Picard's Touchy-Feely World of Empathic Tech," *Wired*, 27 November 2012, www.wired.co.uk /article/emotion-machines.

8. Carmine Gallo, "A Global AI Expert Identifies the Skills You Need to Thrive in the Next 15 Years," *Forbes*, 4 October 2018, www.forbes.com/sites/carmine gallo/2018/10/04/a-global-ai-expert-identifies-the-skills-you-need-to-thrive-in -the-next-15-years.

9. Part of this chapter is a modified version of part of chapter 16 of my book *Against the Flow* (London: Monarch, 2015).

10. This was the title of a paper presented by Joseph Mellichamp at a symposium at Yale University in 1986 on the topic: "Is the Human Mind More Than a Complex Computer?"

SCRIPTURE INDEX

GENERAL INDEX

Seven Days That Divide the World

The Beginning According to Genesis and Science

John C. Lennox

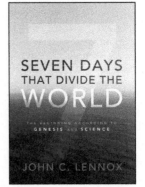

What did the writer of Genesis mean by "the first day"? Is it a literal week or a series of time periods? If I believe that the earth is 4.5 billion years old, am I denying the authority of Scripture?

In response to the continuing controversy over the interpretation of the creation narrative in Genesis, John Lennox proposes a succinct method of reading and interpreting the first chapters of Genesis without discounting either science or Scripture. With examples from history, a brief but thorough exploration of the major interpretations, and a look into the particular significance of the creation of human beings, Lennox suggests that Christians can heed modern scientific knowledge while staying faithful to the biblical narrative. He moves beyond a simple response, insisting that Genesis teaches us far more about the God of Jesus Christ and about God's intention for creation than it does about the age of the earth. With this book, Lennox offers a careful yet accessible introduction to a scientifically savvy, theologically astute, and scripturally faithful interpretation of Genesis.